London Underground

The Jubilee Line

JONATHAN JAMES

TRANSPORT SYSTEMS SERIES, VOLUME 16

Front cover image: A sunny Neasden on 16 June 2023.

Title page image: The tranquil St John's Wood on 1 July 2017.

Contents page image: An original painting of the abandoned Jubilee line concourse at Charing Cross. (Karen Baker)

Back cover image: The iconic station at Canary Wharf on 19 September 2023.

About the Author

Jonathan James has had a lifelong interest in railways and has written more than a dozen books, as well as numerous articles for a variety of transport magazines. His interest is wide-ranging and includes overseas railways, trams, underground railways and steam railways, as well as narrow-gauge and miniature railways.

Having worked in the railway industry in a variety of different roles since 1989, he currently works for the Elizabeth line. He is also a Director of the Narrow Gauge Railway Society.

Published by Key Books
An imprint of Key Publishing Ltd
PO Box 100
Stamford
Lincs PE9 1XQ

www.keypublishing.com

The right of Jonathan James to be identified as the author of this book has been asserted in accordance with the Copyright, Designs and Patents Act 1988 Sections 77 and 78.

Copyright © Jonathan James, 2025

ISBN 978 1 80282 872 6

Typeset by SJmagic DESIGN SERVICES, India.

Contents

Introduction

The Jubilee line started life as the Fleet line, but was renamed to mark Queen Elizabeth II's Silver Jubilee in 1977, although the first stage of the new railway would not open until 1979. The Jubilee line inherited the Stanmore branch from the Bakerloo line, part of which had originally been opened by the Metropolitan Railway. There were grand plans for the Jubilee line, with the new section between Baker Street and Charing Cross being the first stage of a line that would have continued into south-east London. Funding issues, however, prevented substantive progress beyond Charing Cross (although the over-run tunnels did almost reach Aldwych).

Development of the London Docklands began in the 1980s, starting with the area initially served by the Docklands Light Railway (DLR). It soon became clear, however, that the DLR, despite much expansion, would not be able to meet future demand. Several options for enhancing public transport in the London Docklands were explored, including an extension to the Bakerloo line, before the decision was made to extend the Jubilee line.

The Jubilee line's new alignment diverted from Green Park away from Charing Cross towards Westminster and across the river to Southwark and London Bridge. This resulted in the Jubilee line platforms at Charing Cross station being closed to passenger services, although it has been retained for reversing trains. The new extension opened in stages, starting with North Greenwich to Stratford. The remainder of the line was completed later in 1999, ahead of the Millennium Exhibition at the Millennium Dome (now the O2) at North Greenwich.

The extension introduced new technology, including the first use of platform-edge doors on the London Underground. Passive provision, meanwhile, was made for a possible future extension to the Royal Docks. The Jubilee line's relatively recent 1983 tube stock was replaced by a new fleet of 1996-stock trains and a large new depot was constructed at Stratford Market.

My interest in the Jubilee line stems from a visit to London with my late father, who pointed out a construction site sometime in the 1970s.

A number of people have assisted me with this project, including Malcolm Batten, Robert Mitchell, Roy Kenneth and Derek Mulquin. All photographs are by the author unless indicated otherwise. I would also like to thank Tina Clarke and Malcolm Payne from the Transport for London Engineering Office for their help and advice.

Any errors are my own and I welcome any feedback or corrections.

Jonathan James
Chatham, April 2025

The Jubilee line.

Chapter 1

Before the Jubilee Line

The predecessor of today's Jubilee line was constructed in four stages, commencing with the section between Wembley Park and Stanmore, which was opened by the Metropolitan Railway on 10 December 1932. The station at Queensbury opened a couple of years later, on 16 December 1934. Stanmore, Canons Park, Queensbury and Kingsbury all had two platforms each. Initially, trains operated as a shuttle between Stanmore and Wembley Park, with some trains running through to Baker Street over the existing Metropolitan line tracks.

As 'Metroland' continued to grow, the two-track section of railway between Baker Street and Finchley Road became increasingly congested and a constraint to further development. Several options were considered to resolve this issue, but the cost was prohibitive. The solution materialised shortly after the formation of the London Passenger Transport Board in 1933; plans were drawn up for an ambitious programme of works, which included new tube tunnels between Baker Street and Finchley Road to enable some Metropolitan line services to be transferred to the Bakerloo line. Harrow-on-the Hill was considered as a terminus before Stanmore was chosen and confirmed. London Transport's 1935–1940 New Works Programme included other improvements to the Metropolitan line.

The Bakerloo line was opened to Stanmore on 20 November 1939 and took over all stopping services between Stanmore and Finchley Road, enabling Metropolitan line services to be speeded up. The new Bakerloo line tunnels between Finchley Road and Baker Street included stations at Swiss Cottage and St John's Wood (originally to be called Acacia Road), which enabled the closure of the Metropolitan line stations on the two-track section between Finchley Road and Baker Street, at Swiss Cottage, Marlborough Road and Lord's. Marlborough Road and Lord's closed in 1939, followed by Swiss Cottage in 1940. The original intention had been to keep Lord's open for special events, but the station was not retained. The Bakerloo line thus operated with two branches from Baker Street, one to Stanmore and one to Watford Junction.

When Stage 1 of the Jubilee line opened from Baker Street to Charing Cross on 1 May 1979, it adopted the former Bakerloo line service between Stanmore and Baker Street. Further progression of the Jubilee line was not to come until 1999, when it was extended from Green Park to Stratford.

A train of 1938 Tube Stock at Kingsbury on 26 April 1979 when the Stanmore branch was still part of the Bakerloo line. (Malcolm Batten)

The Fleet Line Proposals

The London Plan

The County of London Plan was published in 1943 and set out the strategy for reconstructing London following the end of World War Two, including housing, hospitals, schools, roads and railways.

Building on the initial report, the Railway (London Plan) Committee was established to develop the railway schemes further and included members of the Railway Executive and the London Transport Executive. The Railway (London Plan) Committee published its initial report on 21 January 1946, with the final report published on 3 March 1948. The report proposed several new railway lines numbered 1 to 11, 12A and 12B.

Route 8 later became the genesis of the Victoria line. A number of the other proposals contained elements of what would become the Fleet line proposal, including Route 4, which would have consisted of a new tunnel from Lewisham via Cannon Street, Blackfriars, Aldwych, Piccadilly, Marble Arch, Paddington and Maida Vale to Cricklewood, connecting with the Southern Region line towards Dartford via Blackheath and Bexleyheath at Lewisham and with the LMS lines towards St Albans and Harpenden to the north.

The London Plan Working Party Report

The final *London Plan Working Party Report* was published by the British Transport Commission in 1949. To avoid confusion with the earlier reports, the schemes were given letters instead of numbers. This included a further refinement of Route 8 (now called Route C), which formed the basis for the Victoria line. Elements of what would later become the Fleet line proposal can be seen in Routes D and F.

Route D was a proposed new main-line gauge railway, linking Hackney Downs and Clapton with Victoria via Liverpool Street, Bank, Ludgate Circus, Aldwych, Trafalgar Square and Victoria. This would have connected with the existing lines to Chingford and Enfield Town, which would have been electrified (both routes are now

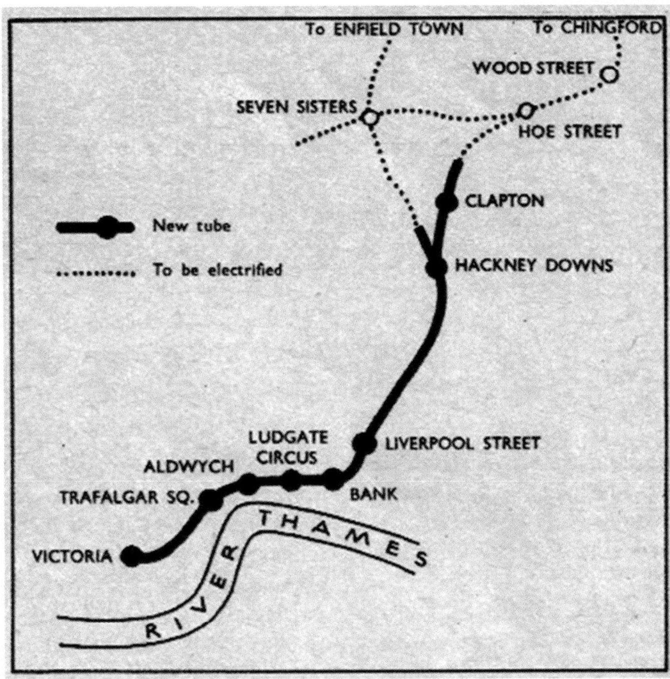

A map showing Route D, from the *London Transport Magazine*, August 1949.

part of the London Overground network). A possible extension beyond Victoria would have taken the route to Knightsbridge, Kensington High Street, Kensington Olympia and then via Ealing and Southall to Yeading Lane. From Victoria, a number of alternatives were considered including a connection to the District line enabling through trains to Wimbledon, Richmond, Hounslow and Heathrow. Route D also has similarities with the proposed Chelsea–Hackney line / Crossrail 2 route.

Route F was a lower priority scheme, again involving the construction of a main-line gauge tunnel between Hither Green and Neasden via Fenchurch Street, Bank, Ludgate Circus, Trafalgar Square, Marble Arch and Marylebone. This new tunnel would have connected with Southern Region services to Sevenoaks and Gillingham (Kent) via Dartford to the south and to High Wycombe, Aylesbury, Berkhamsted and Tring to the north. Routes D and F would have connected at Bank, Ludgate Circus and Trafalgar Square.

Priority was given to developing Route C, which became the Victoria line linking Walthamstow, Victoria and Brixton.

A Railway Plan for London

In 1963, The Transport Planning Working Party for London was established, with British Rail and London Transport working together to develop future proposals for the London rail network.

In March 1965, a report called *A Railway Plan for London* was published. The report proposed a new underground railway, called the Fleet line, between Baker Street and Lewisham via Charing Cross and

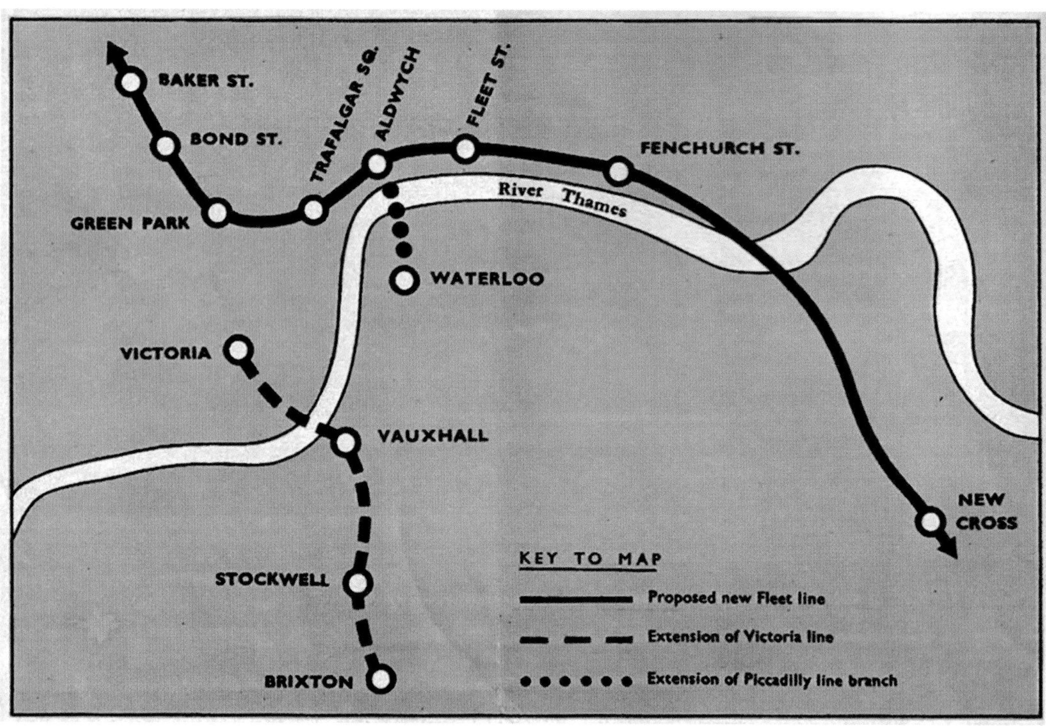

A map from the October 1965 issue of the *London Transport Magazine*, showing three proposed extensions to the Underground network. The first priority was the Piccadilly line extension from Aldwych to Waterloo, which was estimated to cost £4.5 million, with construction expected to commence in 1966. This would have been closely followed by the extension of the Victoria line to Brixton at an estimated cost of £15 million (the Victoria line was already under construction between Walthamstow and Victoria). The Fleet line was the third priority and was estimated to cost around £57 million.

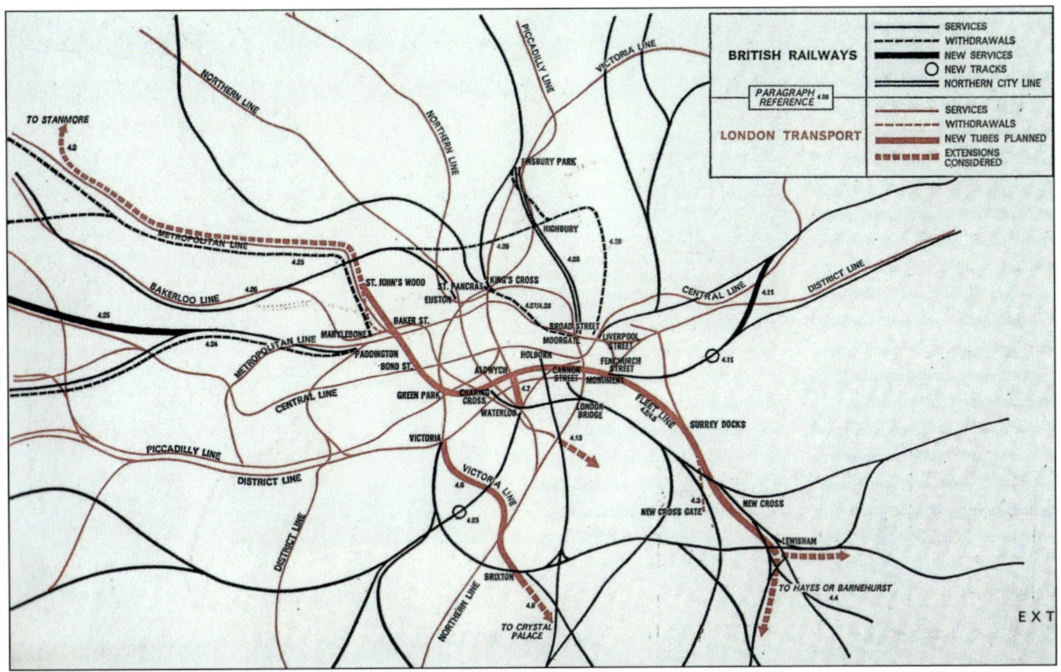

This plan, from the *A Railway Plan for London* report of 1965 shows the Fleet line, including options for extending the line from Lewisham to Hayes (Kent) or Barnehurst. The map also shows a proposed extension of the Victoria line from Brixton to Crystal Palace.

Fenchurch Street. North of Baker Street, the proposed line would take over the existing Bakerloo line service to Stanmore. From Fenchurch Street, the railway would utilise sections of the existing East London line (then part of the Metropolitan line) to reach Lewisham. The East London line would have become a shuttle service between Shoreditch and Surrey Docks (now Surrey Quays), with the New Cross Gate branch abandoned.

In 1972 the Greater London Council (GLC) published a report called *Public Transport in London – A Regional Approach*. The Victoria line had just been completed and construction of the Piccadilly line extension to Heathrow airport had commenced.

The report listed four options for developing the rail network, as follows:

(a) Completion of Fleet line stages 2 and 3 (Charing Cross to Lewisham).
(b) Extension of the Bakerloo line to Peckham via Camberwell.
(c) A new east–west line serving London's Docklands.
(d) A new south–west, north–east line from Wimbledon to Hainault serving Chelsea and Hackney.

Detailed Planning

Detailed planning and surveys then commenced, with construction of the first stage of the Fleet line between Baker Street and Charing Cross expected to be completed by the mid-1970s. The first stage would have provided valuable relief to the overcrowded Bakerloo line section between Baker Street and Charing Cross. The plans were also revised to retain the New Cross Gate branch. The Greater London Transport Group was formed to develop the proposal and secure the necessary funding.

Detailed plans were drawn up to open the Fleet line in four stages. The proposed route was safeguarded to make sure that any subsequent developments were designed to accommodate the future railway.

Stage	Section	Planning Approval Obtained
Stage 1	Baker Street–Charing Cross	25 July 1969
Stage 2	Charing Cross–Fenchurch Street	27 July 1971
Stage 3	Fenchurch Street–New Cross Gate / New Cross	5 August 1971
Stage 3	New Cross–Lewisham	9 August 1972
Stage 4	Lewisham–Addiscombe / Hayes	No specific authority was obtained. Most of the route would have utilised existing railway lines

Funding for Stage 1 was approved in 1971, but the later stages were put on hold to enable consideration of an alternative route to London Docklands.

Funding constraints were also an issue, so further options were considered to reduce costs, including construction of the tunnels from Charing Cross to Fenchurch Street without installing the track or fitting out the stations, so as to protect the route. An extension from Charing Cross to Cannon Street only, or to Cannon Street and Fenchurch Street only, were considered.

Chapter 3

Jubilee Line Stage 1

Construction commenced in February 1972 with the heavy engineering completed by the end of 1975. Twin tunnels were constructed between Baker Street and Charing Cross, including the over-run tunnels that almost reached Aldwych.

At Baker Street, the Bakerloo line branch to Queen's Park and Watford Junction needed to be segregated from the Stanmore branch. The Bakerloo line had three platforms at Baker Street, one Northbound and two Southbound, enabling trains from Stanmore and Watford Junction to be regulated at Baker Street. The former Southbound Bakerloo line platform from the Stanmore branch, was taken over by the Jubilee line. In the opposite direction, a new Northbound Jubilee line platform was constructed. Connecting passageways were constructed to provide interchange between the Bakerloo and Jubilee line platforms and the sub-surface platforms used by the Circle and Metropolitan lines.

Bond Street station needed significant works to enlarge the ticket hall, provide connections with the Central line and construct additional escalators to the Jubilee line platforms. A steel deck was installed at street level to enable road traffic to continue while the new station was constructed beneath. The enlarged station included a new shopping centre. More recently, further changes were made at Bond Street to incorporate the Elizabeth line.

Green Park station required less work, as the ticket hall had already been enlarged as part of the Victoria line works.

The work at Charing Cross involved combining the Bakerloo line station at Trafalgar Square with the Northern line station at Strand. A steel deck was constructed outside Charing Cross main line station to facilitate the work taking place below ground. The construction required the temporary closure of the Northern line station at Strand between 16 June 1973 and 1 May 1979, when it reopened as Charing Cross. To facilitate the construction, a tunnel was constructed beneath Trafalgar Square to a worksite adjacent to the National Gallery; this is now occupied by the Sainsbury Wing, which opened on 9 July 1991.

The work undertaken for Jubilee line Stage 1 included construction of a new Bakerloo line depot at Stonebridge Park, replacing the facilities previously used by the Bakerloo line trains at Stanmore and Neasden.

The sidings at Stanmore were reconstructed to provide ten stabling sidings in place of the original seven. The project funding included new trains for the Fleet line and the new Bakerloo line depot at Stonebridge Park.

New substations were provided at Hays Mews (near Green Park) and Charing Cross, with the line signalled from an existing facility at Finchley Road.

In 1974, the abandoned Piccadilly line platform at Aldwych station was used to create a full-size mock-up of the new Fleet line station at Bond Street.

Shortly before opening, the Fleet line was renamed the Jubilee line, to commemorate the Silver Jubilee of Queen Elizabeth II in 1977.

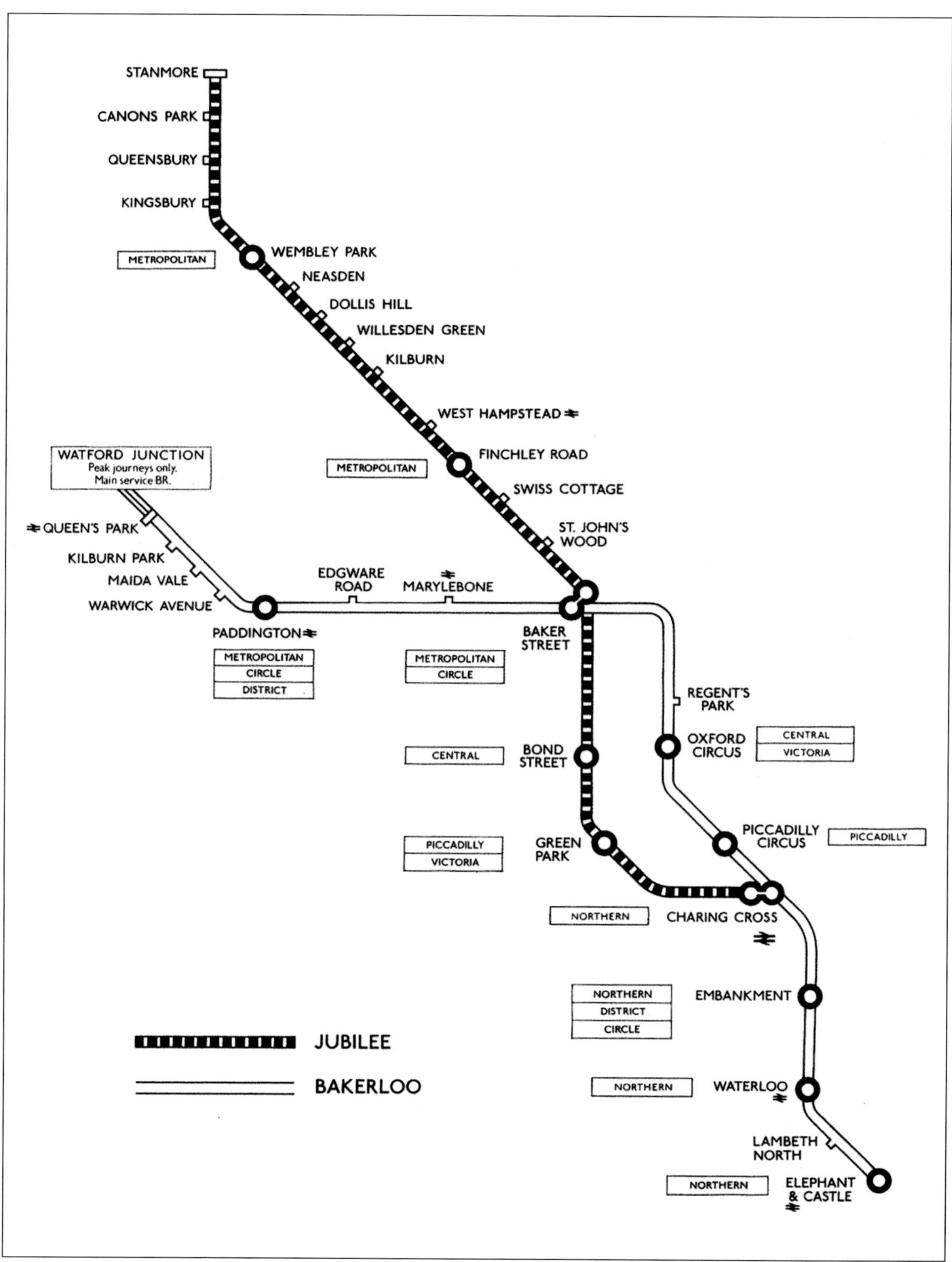

A map produced in 1979 showing the Bakerloo and Jubilee lines.

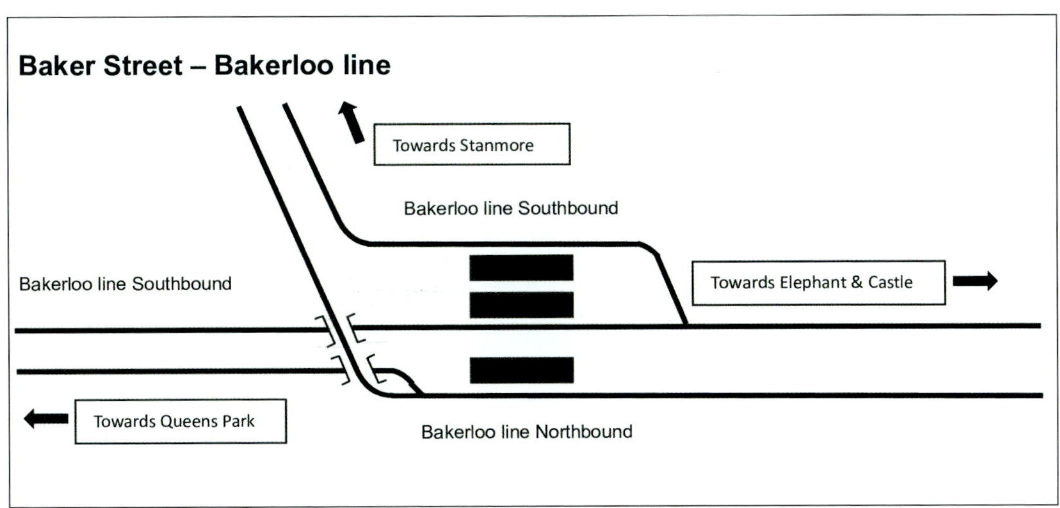

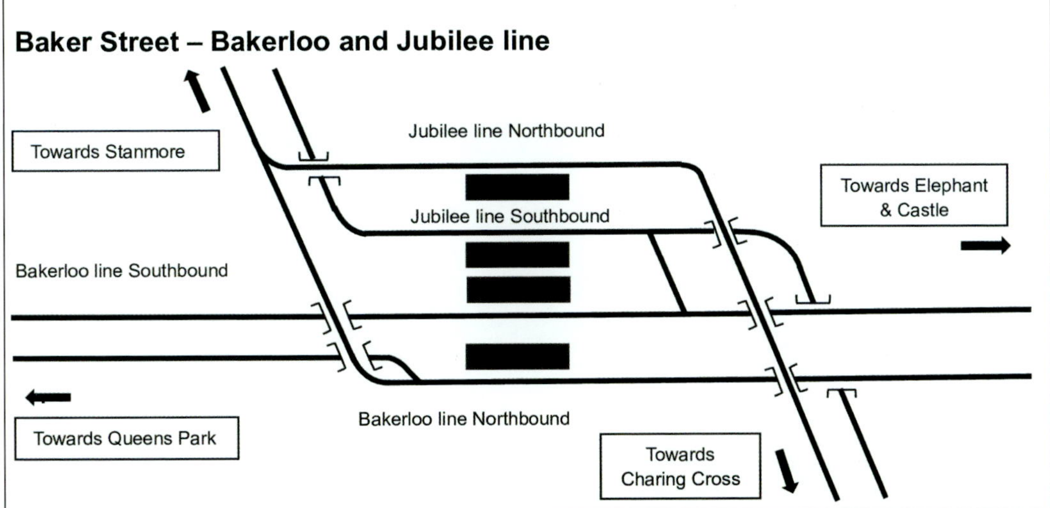

Top: The layout at Baker Street when both the Stanmore and Queen's Park branches formed part of the Bakerloo line.

Above: A new Northbound platform constructed for the Jubilee line enabled the Bakerloo and Jubilee lines to operate independently. Connections remain between the two lines at Baker Street, but they are not used by passenger trains.

Right: A Jubilee line and Bakerloo line timetable was produced for the Jubilee line opening, explaining the new services.

Above: A view of the Fleet line construction site at Witcomb Street in 1976. (Copyright TfL from the London Transport Museum Collection)

Opposite above: The new platforms at Charing Cross under construction in 1978. (Copyright TfL from the London Transport Museum Collection)

Opposite below: The Southbound platform at Charing Cross under construction in 1976. (Copyright TfL from the London Transport Museum Collection)

Above: The temporary steel deck being installed at the junction between Oxford Street and Bond Street to enable construction of the new station at Bond Street in June 1972. (Copyright TfL from the London Transport Museum Collection)

Left: Prince Charles, Prince of Wales (now King Charles III) in the cab of a Jubilee line train at Green Park on opening day, 30 April 1979. (Copyright TfL from the London Transport Museum Collection)

A First Day Cover that was carried on the opening train on 30 April 1979, ahead of public service, which commenced the following day.

A train of 1972 Mark II stock at Charing Cross with a train for Stanmore. (Copyright TfL from the London Transport Museum Collection)

A train of 1983 stock at Charing Cross with a train for Stanmore on 18 April 1986. (Copyright TfL from the London Transport Museum Collection)

Charing Cross station is now served by the Bakerloo and Northern lines. The Jubilee line platforms remain, but are not used for passenger services. This photograph was taken on 23 June 2023.

Chapter 4

Jubilee Line Stages 2, 3 and 4

STAGE 2: CHARING CROSS–FENCHURCH STREET

The running tunnels constructed during Stage 1 of the Jubilee line between Baker Street and Charing Cross extended under the Strand to provide additional rolling-stock stabling capacity.

This also enabled work to commence on Stage 2 without significant impact on the operation of the Stanmore–Charing Cross section. The tunnels almost reached Aldwych, which would have been the first station on Stage 2, providing an interchange with the Piccadilly line branch from Holborn to Aldwych (which closed on 30 September 1994).

The second station would have been at Ludgate Circus, where a parcel of land was reserved for the future extension. A passageway was constructed in preparation. This is now the site of City Thameslink station.

From Ludgate Circus, the line would have served Cannon Street, providing an interchange with British Rail as well as the Circle and District lines. The station here would have been located between Cannon Street and Monument, providing a connection to Monument station. An underground station box was constructed in front of Cannon Street station, while the foundations of the Bush Lane House office development were designed to accommodate the future extension.

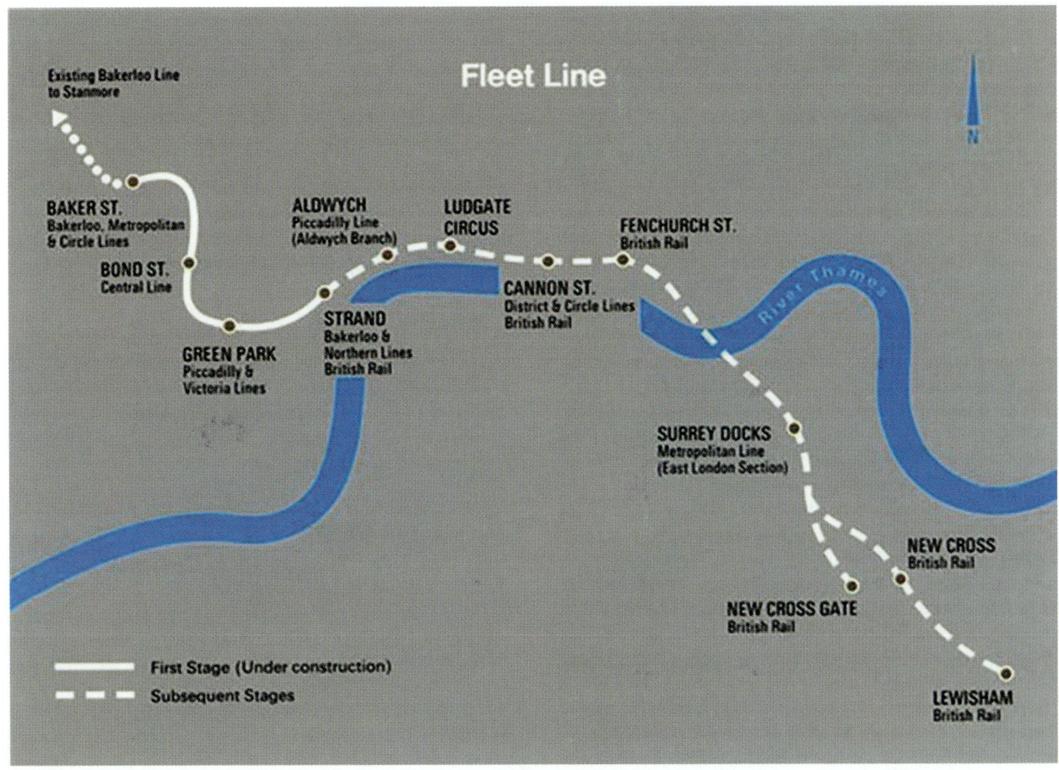

A map of the proposed Fleet line from the *1971 London Transport Annual Report*.

The final stop on Stage 2 was intended to be Fenchurch Street, which remains the only main line terminal in London without a direct Underground connection. A turnback siding would have been constructed beyond Fenchurch Street station, but the crossovers west of Charing Cross would not have been used on a regular basis once the Jubilee line was extended eastwards to Fenchurch Street and beyond.

All the stations on Stage 2 would have been provided with two platforms. Substations would have been constructed at Ludgate Circus and Fenchurch Street. Fan shafts, meanwhile, would have been located at Southampton Street (between Charing Cross and Aldwych), Bouverie Street (between Aldwych and Ludgate Circus) and Great Trinity Lane (between Ludgate Circus and Cannon Street).

Rather optimistically, ceremonial 'spade in ground' events took place on 4 April 1978 at Strand and 26 April 1978 at Aldwych.

Various options were explored for reducing the cost of Stage 2, such as removing the connection to the Piccadilly line at Aldwych or terminating the line at Cannon Street.

Charing Cross (Strand) to Aldwych

The Fleet line tunnels would have followed the Strand, running alongside the Lyceum Theatre before passing beneath St Mary Le Strand church and then crossing the Piccadilly line branch from Holborn at a right angle.

Aldwych station still exists and is often used by film companies. Had the Fleet line been extended beyond Charing Cross, an interchange would have been built with the Piccadilly line branch from Holborn, which seems likely to have survived, along with the proposed extension to Waterloo. Unfortunately, this was not the case, and it was the prohibitive cost of replacing the lifts that led to the closure of Aldwych in 1994. Only the west platform at Aldwych was used by Piccadilly line trains between 1914 and closure, the other platform being used to create mock-ups of station designs, including the Fleet line station at Bond Street. The station building still carries the original station name of Strand. This picture was taken on 23 January 2016. The London Transport Museum operates Hidden London tours to the former Piccadilly line platforms at Aldwych and Holborn.

Aldwych

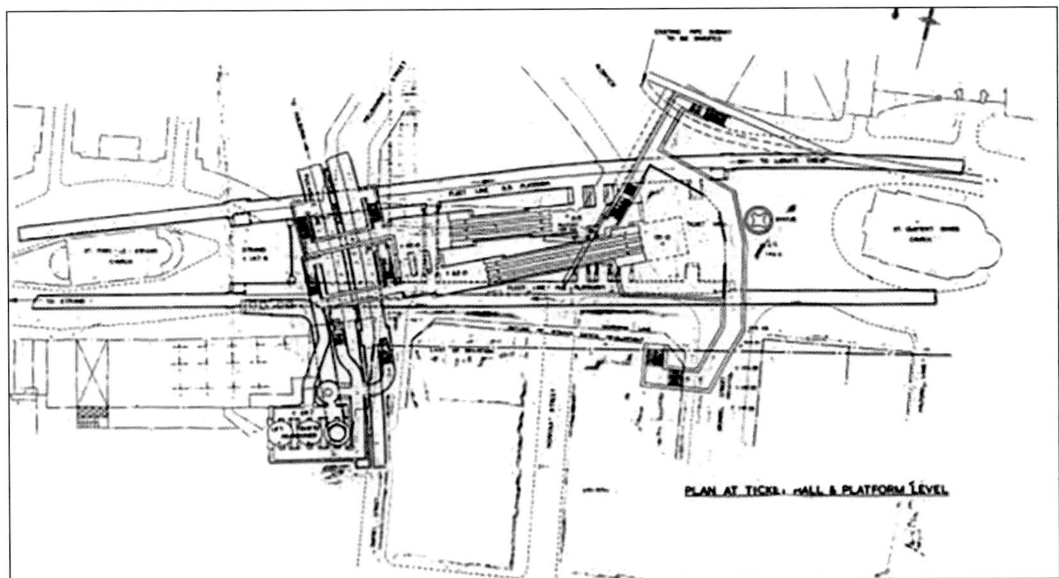

This plan shows Aldwych station, with the Fleet line platforms located to the east side, and the escalators from the platforms passing close to Australia House (now called the Australian High Commission). A new ticket hall would have been built beneath Strand and Arundel Street for the Fleet line and Piccadilly line. Escalators would have led from the new booking hall to both the Fleet line and Piccadilly line platforms. (Copyright TfL from the TfL Engineering Records Collection)

Ludgate Circus

Investigations were undertaken along the length of the Fleet line / River line route, including trial boreholes to gain a detailed understanding of the soil conditions.

In 1974/75, some exploratory works were undertaken on the corner of Bouverie Street and Temple Lane, just west of the proposed Fleet line station at Ludgate Circus. The works would have been utilised as a ventilation shaft for the Fleet line had it been completed.

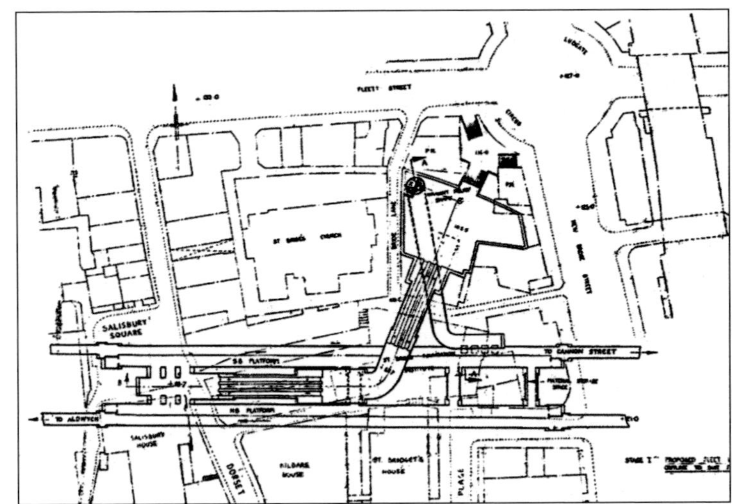

This plan shows the layout at Ludgate Circus, including the two banks of three escalators that would have led to the station entrance on the south-west corner of Ludgate Circus. (Copyright TfL from the TfL Engineering Records Collection)

Above left and above right: The partly constructed Fleet line ventilation shaft at Bouverie Street near Ludgate Circus. (Roy Kenneth)

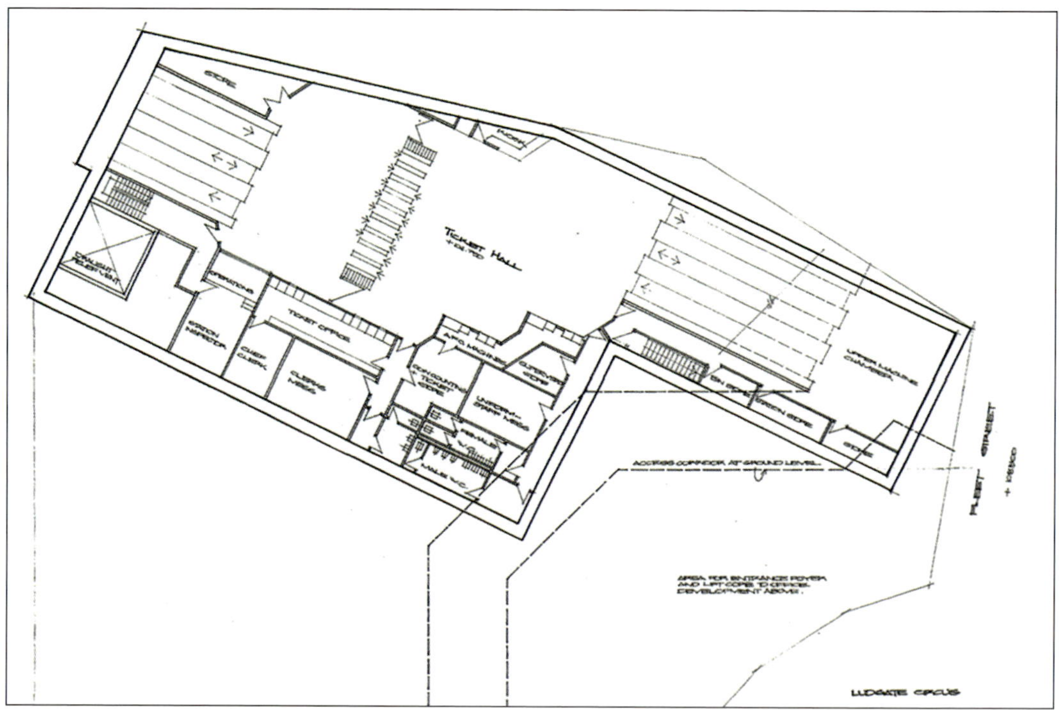

This later plan, dating from 1979, shows the amended booking hall layout at the junction between Fleet Street and Ludgate Circus. (Copyright TfL from the TfL Engineering Records Collection)

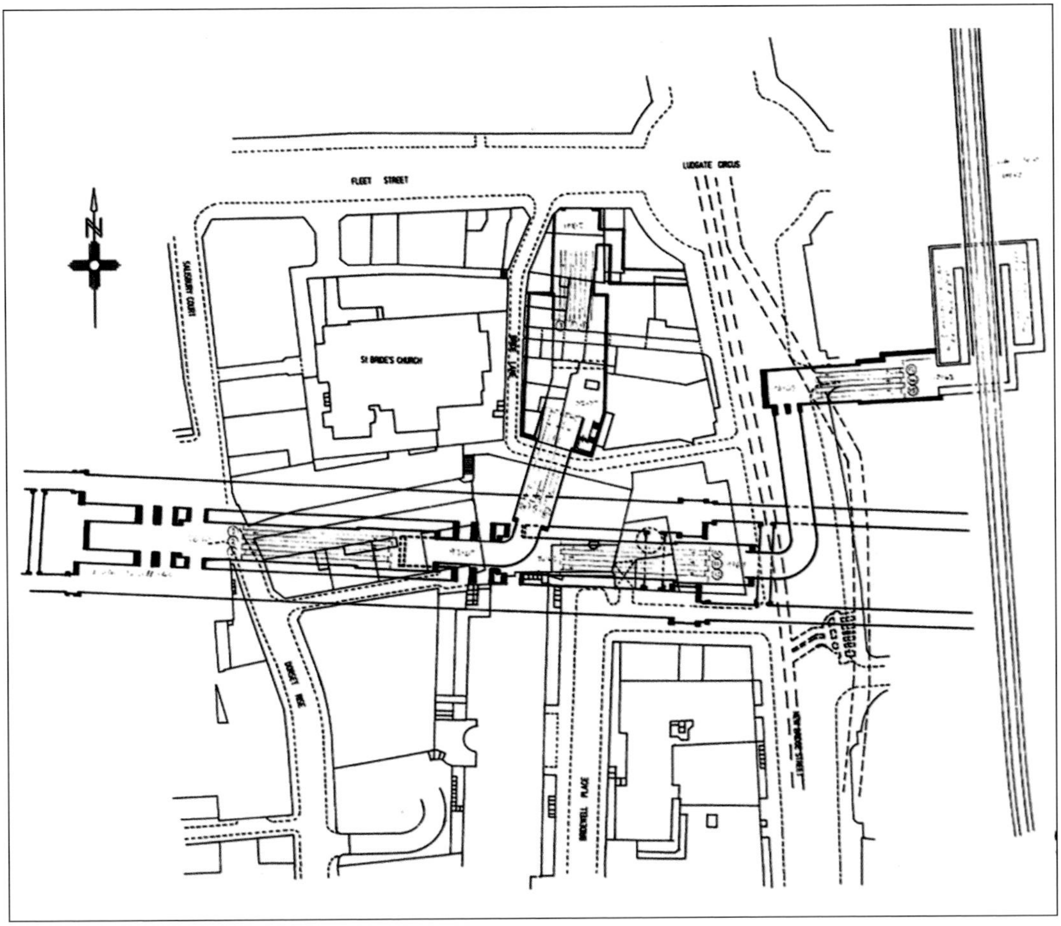

This plan shows a proposed link to the adjacent British Rail station (now City Thameslink), which is shown to the right-hand side of the drawing, with the Fleet line crossing at a right angle. (Copyright TfL from the TfL Engineering Records Collection)

Cannon Street

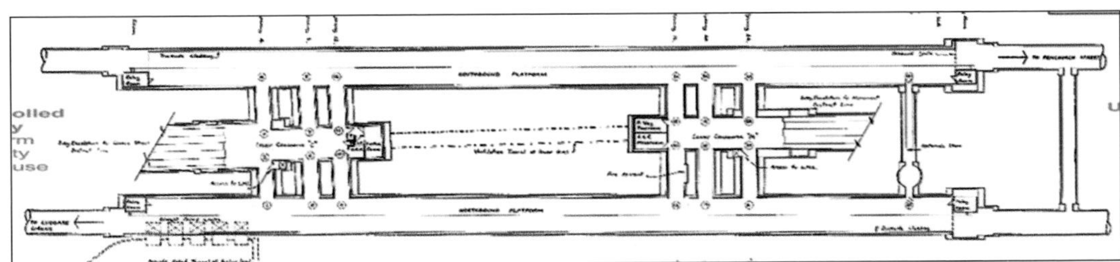

This plan dates from 1973 and shows the platform layout at Cannon Street. There would have been two entrances to the station, one from Cannon Street and the other from Monument station. Three escalators would have led to Cannon Street and two to Monument. (Copyright TfL from the TfL Engineering Records Collection)

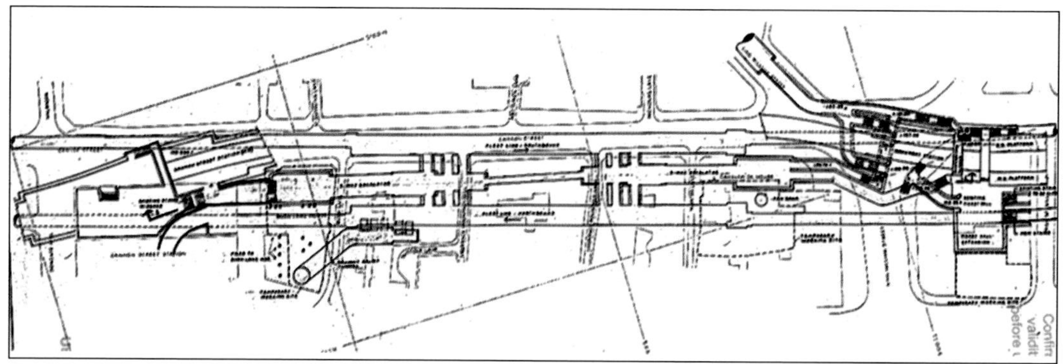

This plan also dates from 1973 and shows the tunnel layout at Cannon Street. The escalators at the Cannon Street end of the station would have connected to the Circle and District line station, while the stairs connecting the Circle and District line booking hall to Cannon Street main line station would have been widened. The Bush Lane House office development is shown below the Cannon Street entrance. A small Underground station box was constructed between the front of Cannon Street main line station and the foundations of Bush Lane House, in preparation for the future Fleet line. (Copyright TfL from the TfL Engineering Records Collection)

Fenchurch Street

The early proposals envisaged three platforms at Fenchurch Street, but this was later amended to two.

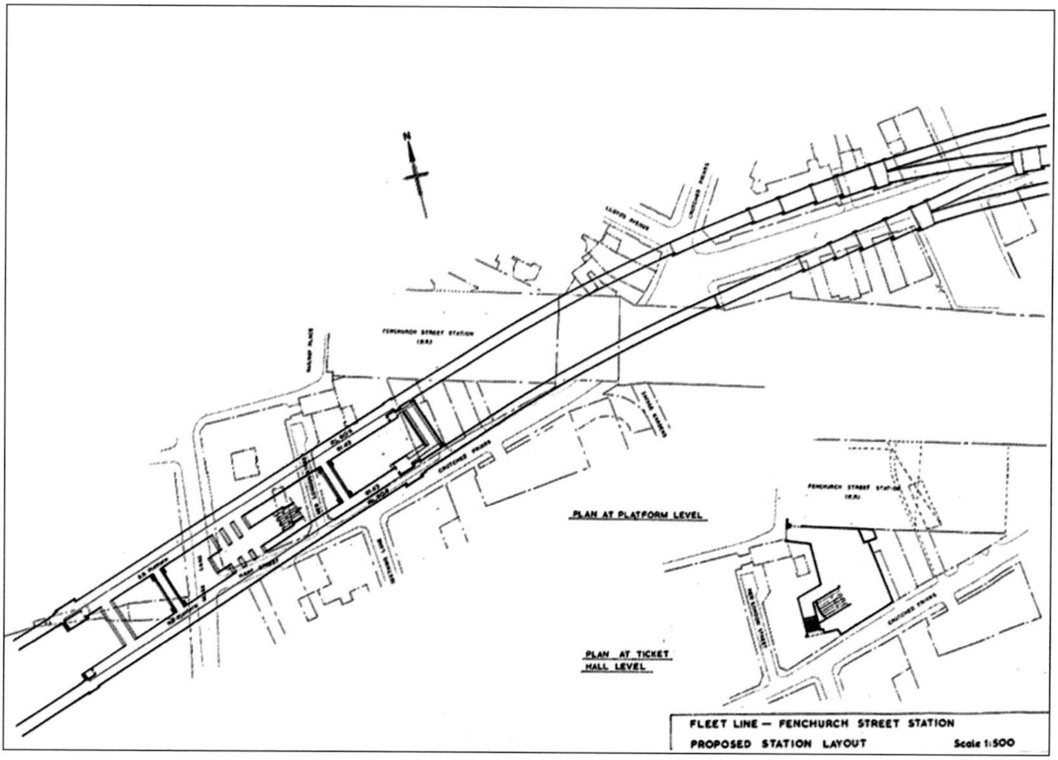

This drawing, dating from 1975, shows the tunnel layout, including the junction to the central turnback siding in the top right corner. (Copyright TfL from the TfL Engineering Records Collection)

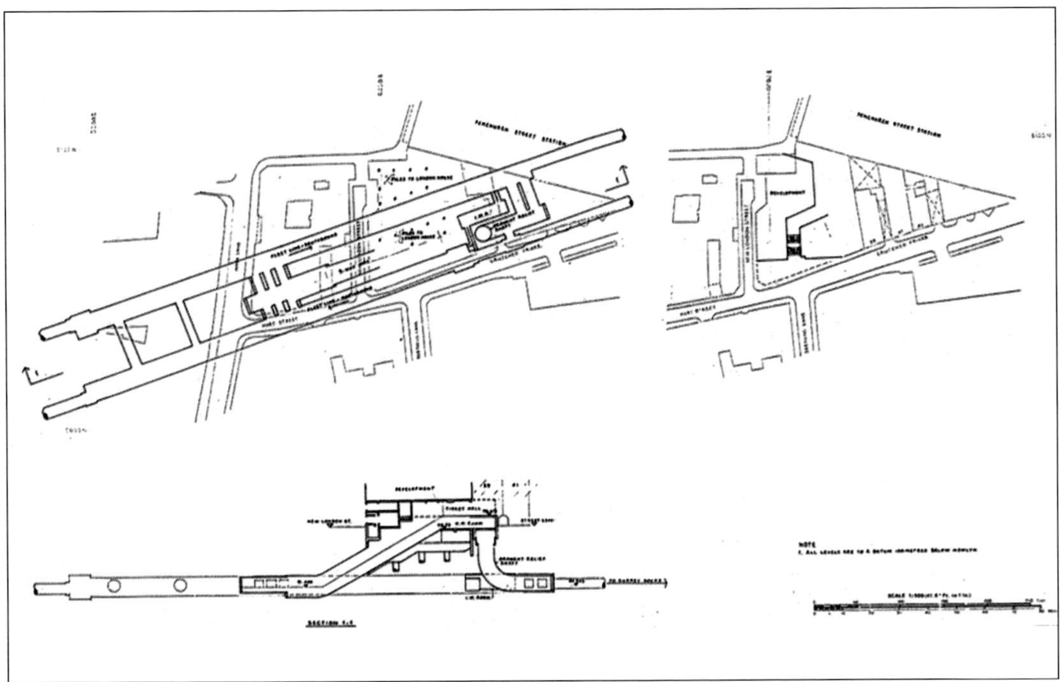

This drawing dates from 1973 and shows the proposed Fleet line station, which would have been constructed partly beneath London House. Three escalators would have connected to the station. The entrance to the Fleet line station would have been directly opposite the entrance to Fenchurch Street main line station. (Copyright TfL from the TfL Engineering Records Collection)

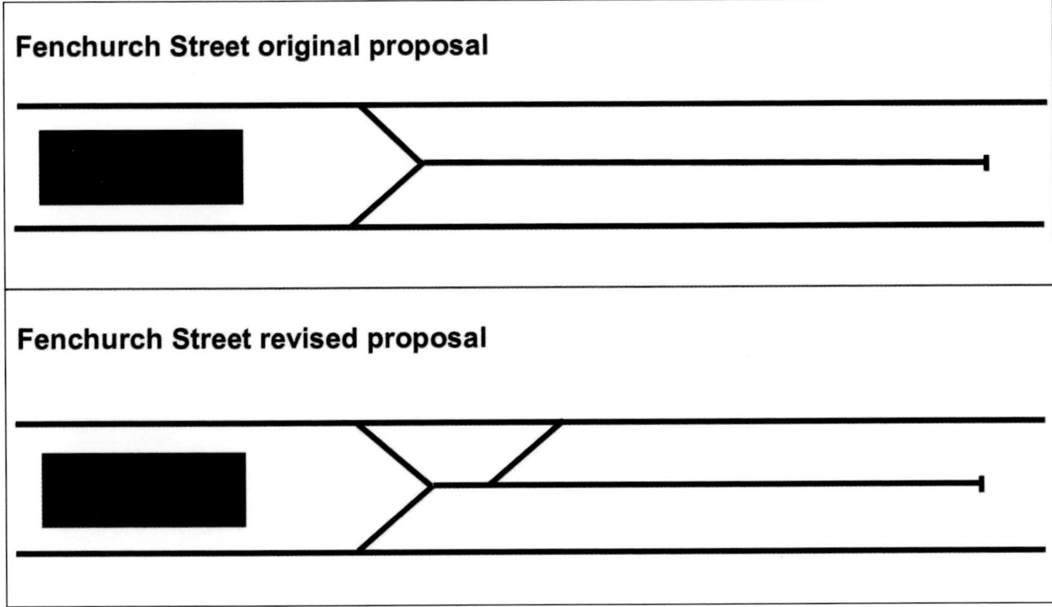

Fenchurch Street would have been provided with a turnback siding, enabling trains from the Stanmore direction to reverse at Fenchurch Street. A revised plan added a crossover to permit trains to cross between the two running tunnels without the need to reverse.

STAGE 3: FENCHURCH STREET–NEW CROSS GATE / LEWISHAM

Two substations would have been constructed at Surrey Docks and Brookhill Road in Lewisham. A fan shaft would have been located at Royal Mint Street, between Fenchurch Street and Surrey Docks, along with an emergency escape and draught relief shaft at Wapping and a relief shaft at New Cross.

Trains would have surfaced just north of Surrey Docks station (now Surrey Quays), with Fleet line services using the current East London line (London Overground) platforms at Surrey Docks, with the East London line terminating in a disused bay platform on the east side of the station. The East London line itself would have become a shuttle service between Shoreditch and Surrey Docks. A new depot would have been constructed beyond Surrey Docks station, close to the current London Overground Silwood sidings site. Services would have split here, with one branch taking over the East London line route to New Cross Gate and terminating at a single platform.

The single-track New Cross branch would need to be doubled to accommodate the increased service levels, achieved through the construction of a single-bore tunnel from just beyond Canal Junction to just outside Lewisham. This arrangement would have resulted in the Northbound platform at New Cross being underground, with the existing surface platform utilised for Southbound trains. The Southbound line would have entered a tunnel just beyond New Cross station, before meeting the Northbound line just before Lewisham. Scissor crossovers would have been provided outside Lewisham station, which would have had two underground platforms. An earlier 1969 scheme proposed a reversing siding beyond the two platforms at Lewisham, rather than the scissor crossovers that were later proposed. A section of experimental tunnel would have been utilised at New Cross.

Limited work was undertaken on Stage 3, over and above surveys and boreholes, plus the purchase of some land at Lewisham.

In 1978 consideration was given to re-routing Stage 3 between Fenchurch Street and Surrey Docks to enable an intermediate station to be built at St Katharine Dock, which was being redeveloped at the time. Another option was to use the East London line's Thames Tunnel between Wapping and Rotherhithe to save costs, with the East London line further curtailed.

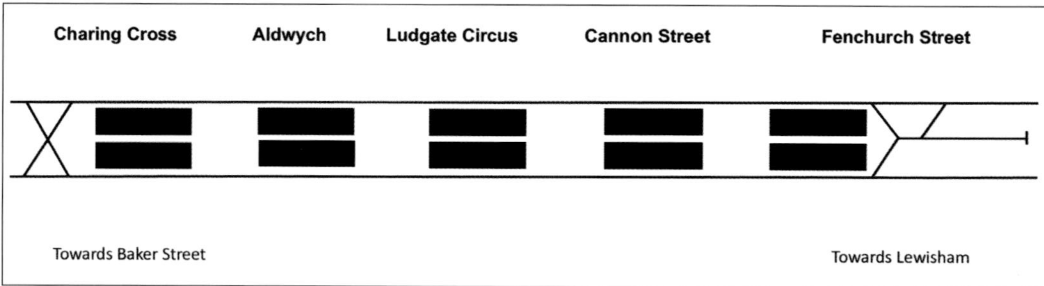

Above and below: **A simplified track layout from Charing Cross to Lewisham.**

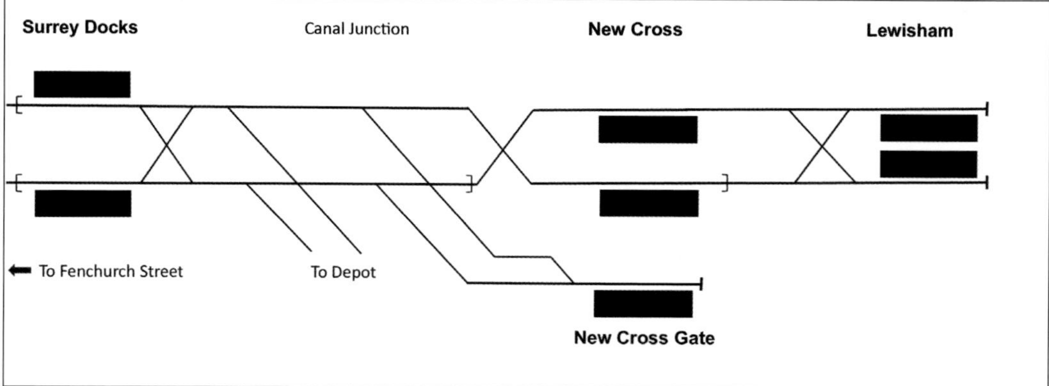

Surrey Docks

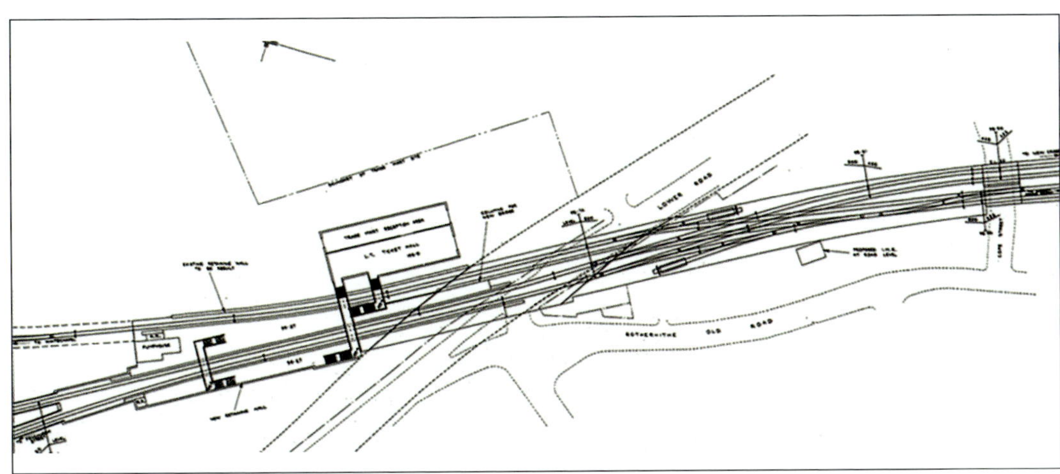

This drawing dates from 1975 and shows the layout at Surrey Docks (now Surrey Quays). The Fleet line from Fenchurch Street is bottom left, with the single-track East London line above (now part of the London Overground Windrush line). A disused platform at Surrey Docks would have been reinstated for use by East London line trains, while the Fleet line would have utilised the existing platforms. To the right of the drawing, the upper two tracks would have continued towards New Cross and New Cross Gate, while the lower pair of tracks would have led to Surrey Docks Depot. (Copyright TfL from the TfL Engineering Records Collection)

Surrey Quays station looking towards Canada Water on 31 July 2023. Stage 3 of the Fleet line would have seen East London line services terminating in the disused bay platform to the right of this view. The tracks shown in this view would have been used by the Fleet line.

The same location on 31 July 2023, but this time looking towards New Cross. East London Line services would have terminated in the disused bay platform, located behind the hoardings on the left of this view, had Stage 3 of the Fleet line progressed. The existing platforms would have been used by Fleet line services.

The New Cross Experimental Tunnel

An experimental section of tunnel was built in New Cross, along the proposed route of the Northbound Fleet line tunnel. The main purpose was to test a new type of tunnelling machine, suitable for digging through water-bearing gravel. This was known as a Bentonite Shield.

The tunnelling machine was delivered to site on 12 December 1971, with work commencing on 24 February 1972; access was provided from a 19.6m-deep shaft. After completion, the experimental cutting head was left behind in the tunnel.

The Bentonite Shield was an evolution of the tunnelling method used to dig through unstable ground which involved using compressed air to retain the loose material until the tunnel lining could be installed. This often resulted, however, in workers' experiencing medical issues akin to 'the bends' suffered by divers, due to working with compressed air.

The Bentonite Shield reduced such effects on the workers by pressurising the front of the cutting head, using a clay slurry to seal the tunnel before the installation of the tunnel rings. The trial tunnel was a success and engendered confidence in this method of tunnelling.

This particular tunnel, hidden below New Cross, is 144m long. Regular surveys are carried out to inspect its condition.

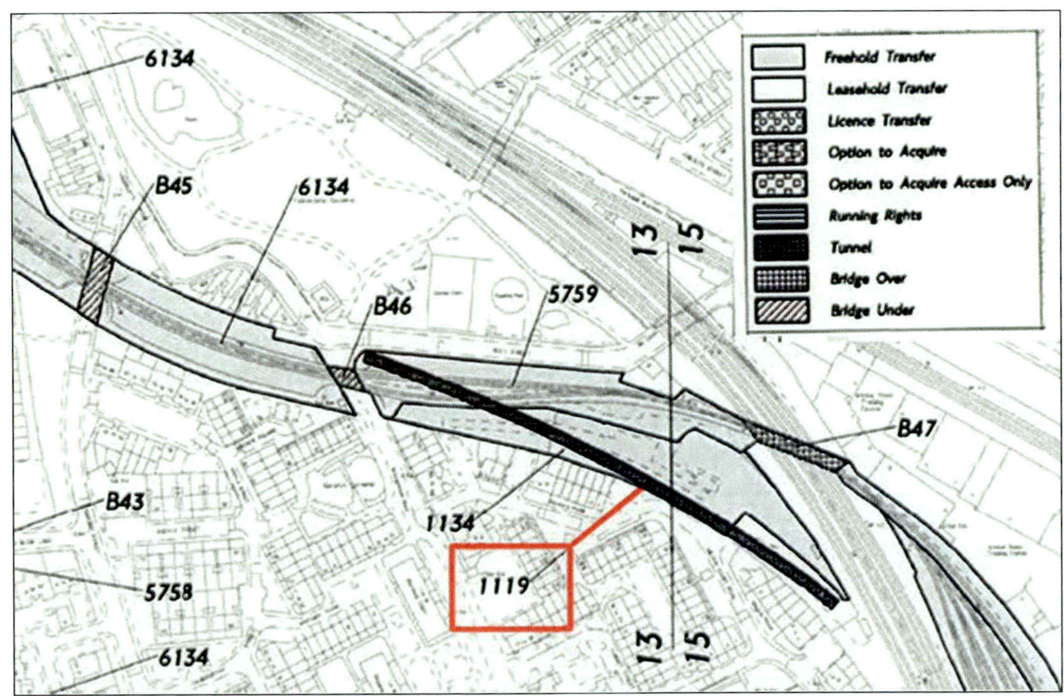

A plan showing the alignment of the experimental tunnel near New Cross. (Copyright TfL from the TfL Engineering Records Collection)

The experimental tunnel at New Cross. (Copyright TfL Engineering Records Collection)

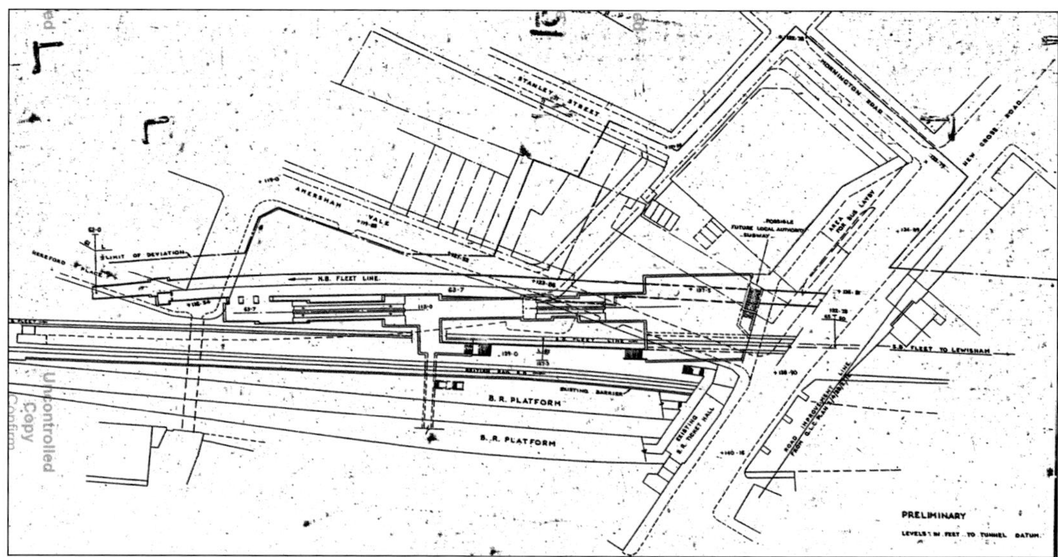

This drawing of New Cross shows the Northbound Fleet line platform in a tunnel, with the Southbound line on the surface, parallel with the two British Rail island platforms. (Copyright TfL from the TfL Engineering Records Collection)

New Cross / New Cross Gate

A new depot would have been constructed just beyond Surrey Docks station, before the routes to New Cross and New Cross Gate diverged at Canal Junction. New Cross Gate station would have been largely unchanged, while at New Cross the Northbound line would have been underground, utilising the experimental tunnel. The Southbound line would have remained on the surface, before joining the Northbound line in a tunnel through to Lewisham.

Lewisham

Lewisham station would have had two platforms, with crossovers at the New Cross end of the station. The overrun tunnels would have extended to Albion Way in preparation for the next stage to Hayes and Addiscombe.

STAGE 4: LEWISHAM–HAYES AND ADDISCOMBE

A number of routes were considered for Stage 4, including an extension via Grove Park and Bromley North to Biggin Hill airport.

The final Stage 4 route was from Lewisham via Catford Bridge to Hayes and Addiscombe. Other than the connection to the Fleet line tunnels at Lewisham, the route would have used existing British Rail tracks.

The Addiscombe branch has since been closed, with some of the route used by the Croydon Tramlink network.

Proposed Services

Several timetable options were explored, with one example summarised below:

Stage 1 (Stanmore–Charing Cross)

Section (Peak Hours)	Frequency (Trains Per Hour)
Stanmore	12
Wembley Park	18
Willesden Green	24
Charing Cross	24

Stages 1 to 3 (Charing Cross–Fenchurch Street and Lewisham)

Section	Monday to Friday (Trains Per Hour)			Sunday (Trains Per Hour)	
	Peaks	Daytime	Evenings	Before 10.30	After 10.30
Stanmore	16	4	3	4	3
Wembley Park	16	8	6	4	6
West Hampstead–Fenchurch Street	24	16	12	8	12
Surrey Docks	24	8	8	8	8
New Cross Gate	8	4	4	4	4
Lewisham	16	4	4	4	4

Stages 1 to 4 (Charing Cross–New Cross Gate, Hayes and Addiscombe via Fenchurch Street and Lewisham)

Section	Monday to Friday (Trains Per Hour)		
	Peaks	Daytime	Evenings
Stanmore	15	5	4
Wembley Park	22½	10	8
Willesden Green	30	20	8
West Hampstead	30	20	16
Fenchurch Street	30	20	16
Surrey Docks	30	20	16
New Cross Gate	6	4	3
Lewisham	24	16	12
Catford Bridge	24	16	12
Elmers End	18	8	6
Addiscombe	6	4	3
Hayes	12	4	3

Chapter 5

The River Line Proposal

The 1974 London Rail Study (*The Barran Report*)

In February 1973, Sir David Barran was appointed by the Greater London Council (GLC) and the Ministry of Transport to investigate the development of rail services in London. *The London Rail Study* was published in November 1974 and is often referred to as *The Barran Report*.

The Barran Report considered several rail schemes, including a traditional tube line linking Wimbledon to Hainault, referred to at the time as the Chelsea–Hackney line and, more recently, Crossrail 2. The proposed line would have connected Waterloo, Aldwych and Holborn, including an interchange with Stage 2 of the Fleet line at Aldwych.

The report also explored both the Fleet line and River line options. Stage 1 of the Fleet line was already under construction between Baker Street and Charing Cross and it was assumed that Stage 2 from Charing Cross to Fenchurch Street would also be completed, at an estimated cost of £50 million.

Also mentioned was the completion of Fleet line Stage 3, which already had planning approval, as well as Stage 4. It was estimated that completion of Stages 3 and 4 would cost £86 million.

The River line was developed as an alternative option to the original Fleet line route beyond Fenchurch Street. At this point in time, plans were being drawn up for the redevelopment of London's docklands, with the River line intended to proceed onwards through this area to connect with the large housing development at Thamesmead, across the river. Circumstances have ensured that even now, Thamesmead still lacks a railway station, although there do now exist proposals for an extension of the Docklands Light Railway from Beckton to Thamesmead.

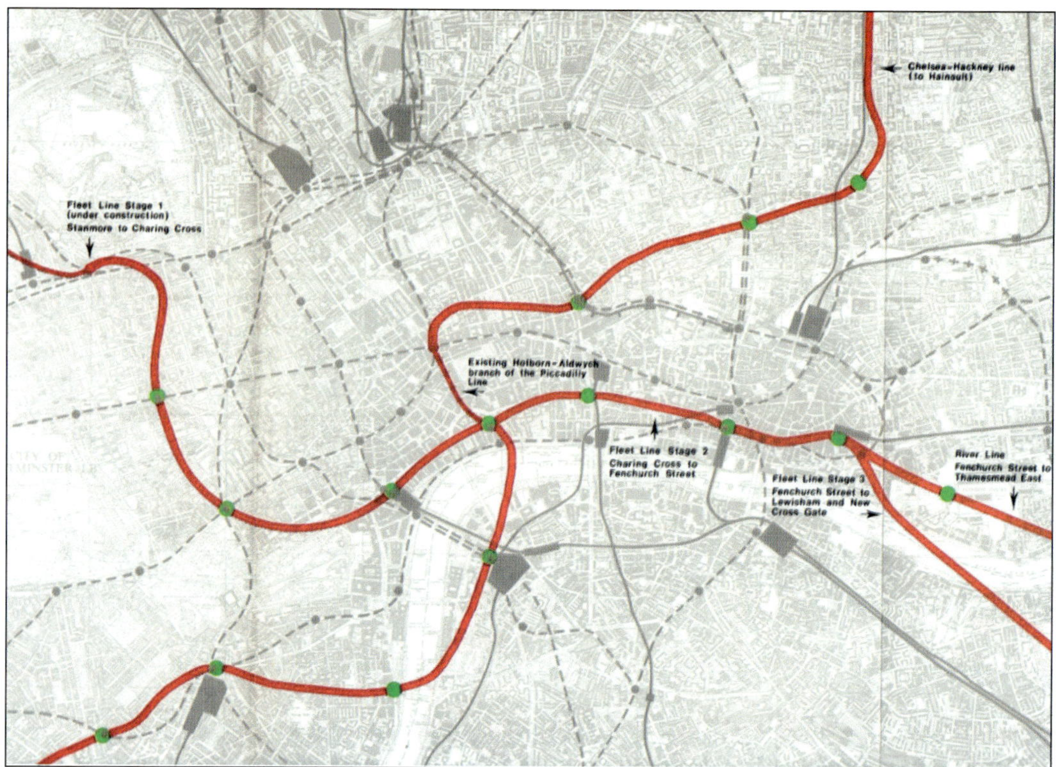

A map from the 1974 London Rail Study, showing the Fleet and River line proposals (left to right) and the proposed Chelsea–Hackney line (top to bottom), including the proposed interchange at Aldwych.

Two River line options were considered as follows:

- **River line North** – This would have commenced at Fenchurch Street, with stops at Stepney East (now Limehouse), Poplar, Custom House, Beckton and Thamesmead. Much of the route would have utilised disused railway alignments (and some of it later came under the auspices of the Docklands Light Railway). The cost was estimated to be £90 million.
- **River line South** – Also commencing at Fenchurch Street, the line would have served Surrey Docks, Isle of Dogs, North Greenwich, Custom House, Woolwich Arsenal and Thamesmead. The cost was estimated to be £110 million.

Some documents also referred to the line as the Thames line.

The report recommended the following rail projects in priority order:

- **Priority A** – The route from Fenchurch Street to Thamesmead via Woolwich Arsenal alongside a low-cost British Rail orbital scheme.
- **Priority B** – Several British Rail electrification projects, including the north–south link via Snow Hill (which later became the Thameslink project) as well as the Chelsea–Hackney line.
- **Priority C** – The lower priority schemes included the extension of the Fleet line to Lewisham, Addiscombe and Hayes, subject to a suitable business case.

Between 1976 and 1978, detailed surveys were undertaken along the route from Fenchurch Street to Thamesmead, including the drilling of boreholes in the interest of evaluating the ground conditions.

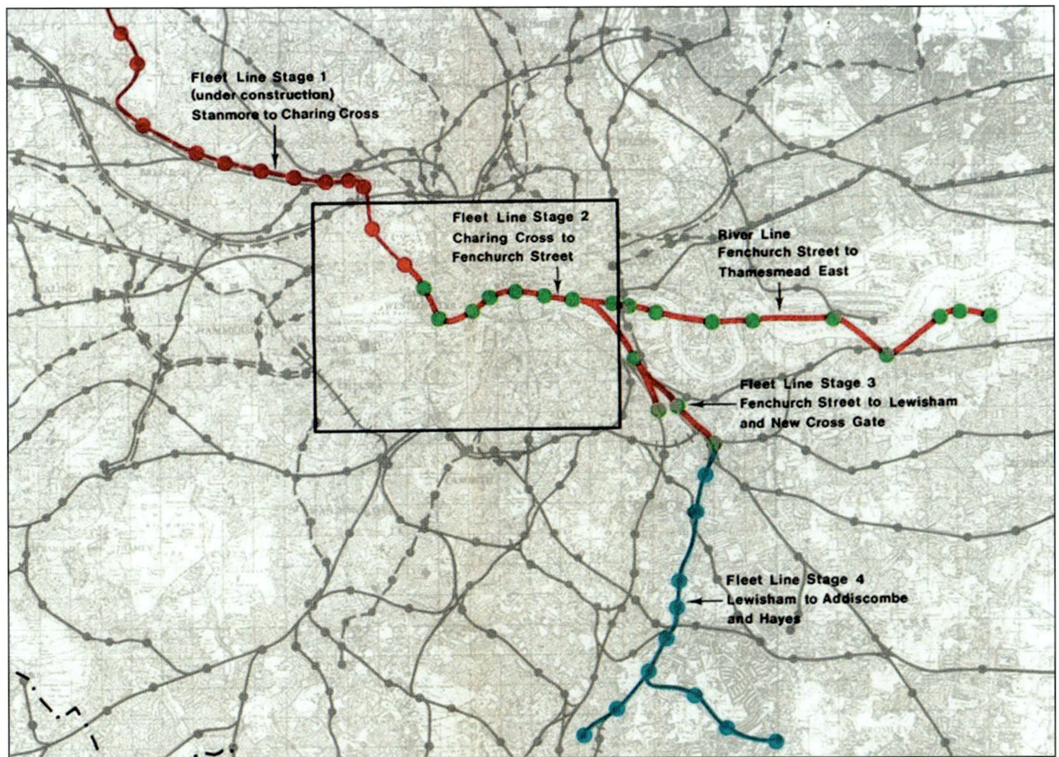

The Fleet line and River line proposals from the 1974 London Rail Study, including the proposed Fleet line Stage 4 (in blue) and the River line towards Thamesmead East.

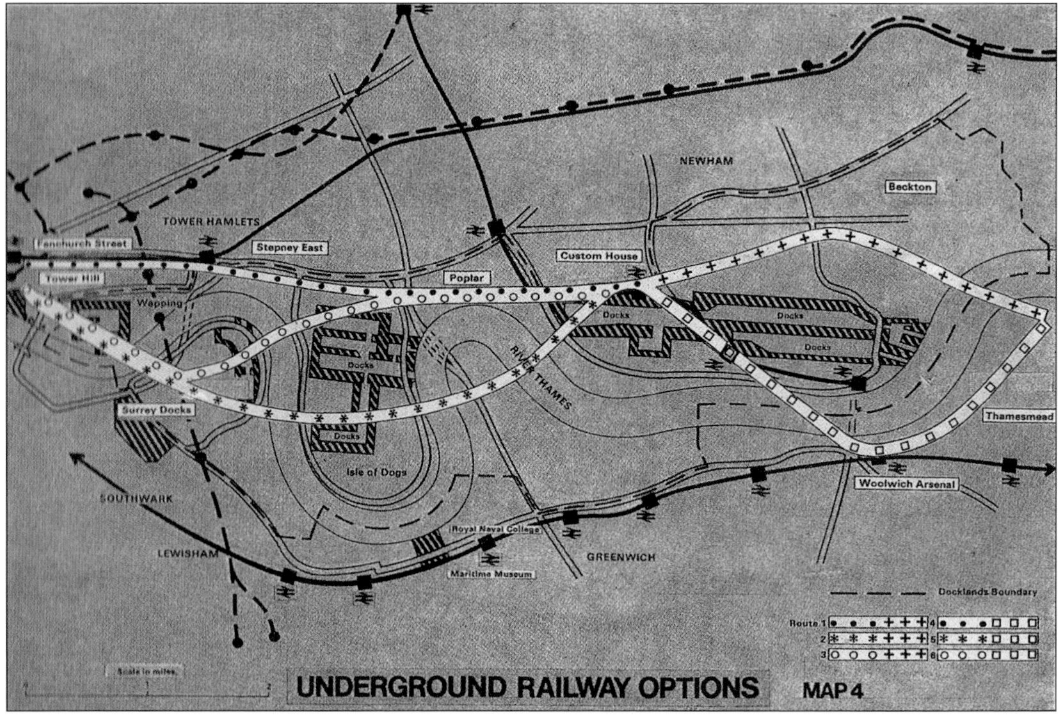

This plan was produced by the Docklands Joint Committee in 1974, outlining potential rail options.

Docklands Joint Committee and the 1976 Docklands Strategic Plan

The Docklands Joint Committee considered six underground railway options for serving London's docklands. In 1976, consideration was given to constructing a main-line gauge single-bore tunnel linking North Woolwich with Woolwich Arsenal, which in the short-term would have enabled British Rail to operate a Stratford to Woolwich Arsenal service, ahead of the River line taking over the route at a later date.

A Working Party was set up to investigate the options, which included a tunnel between Silvertown and Woolwich Arsenal or a tunnel between Custom House and Woolwich Arsenal. This would have included electrification of the British Rail line between Stratford, West Ham and Woolwich Arsenal. A new interchange was also proposed at West Ham.

The British Rail service would have been cut back to Custom House when the Jubilee line was extended to Thamesmead. A second tube tunnel would have been built alongside the main-line gauge tunnel, with both tunnels used by the River line.

1978 Proposal

The Greater London Council put forward a proposal to host the Olympic Games in the Royal Docks, which would have relied upon (and justified) the River line extension.

In 1978, another option emerged, for an express Jubilee line extension from Charing Cross to Thamesmead with stations at Cannon Street, Fenchurch Street, Surrey Docks, Millwall (on the Isle of Dogs), Custom House and Beckton. Primarily designed to reduce costs, this particular plan would have removed the other intermediate stations.

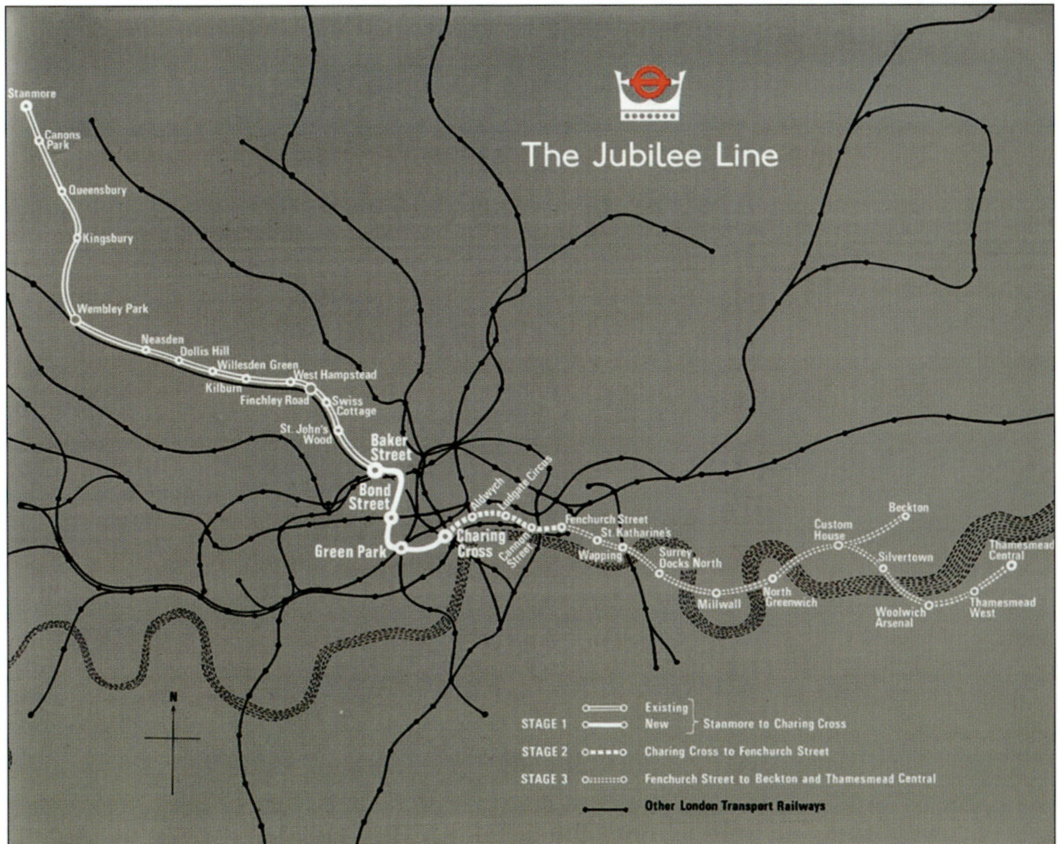

This map was included in the brochure produced for the Jubilee line opening on 30 April 1979, showing the route to Thamesmead Central with a branch from Custom House to Beckton.

The London Transport Annual Report of 1978 proposed a route from Fenchurch Street to Thamesmead Central via St Katharine's Dock, Wapping, Surrey Docks North, Millwall (on the Isle of Dogs), North Greenwich, Custom House, Silvertown, Woolwich Arsenal and Thamesmead West. The option of diverting the proposed line to serve Beckton was considered, but the map included in the final report suggested a branch from Custom House to Beckton, primarily to serve the depot site, although a station may have been included.

1979 Proposals

A further proposal was put forward in 1979, outlining two alternative routes. The first was from Fenchurch Street to Thamesmead Central via St Katharine's, Wapping, Surrey Docks North, Millwall, North Greenwich, Custom House, Silvertown, Woolwich Arsenal and Thamesmead West. The second route (also earmarked as a possible busway or light rail line) would have run from Fenchurch Street to Thamesmead Central via Shadwell, Stepney East (since renamed Limehouse), Poplar, Custom House (interchanging with the British Rail North Woolwich branch) and Beckton.

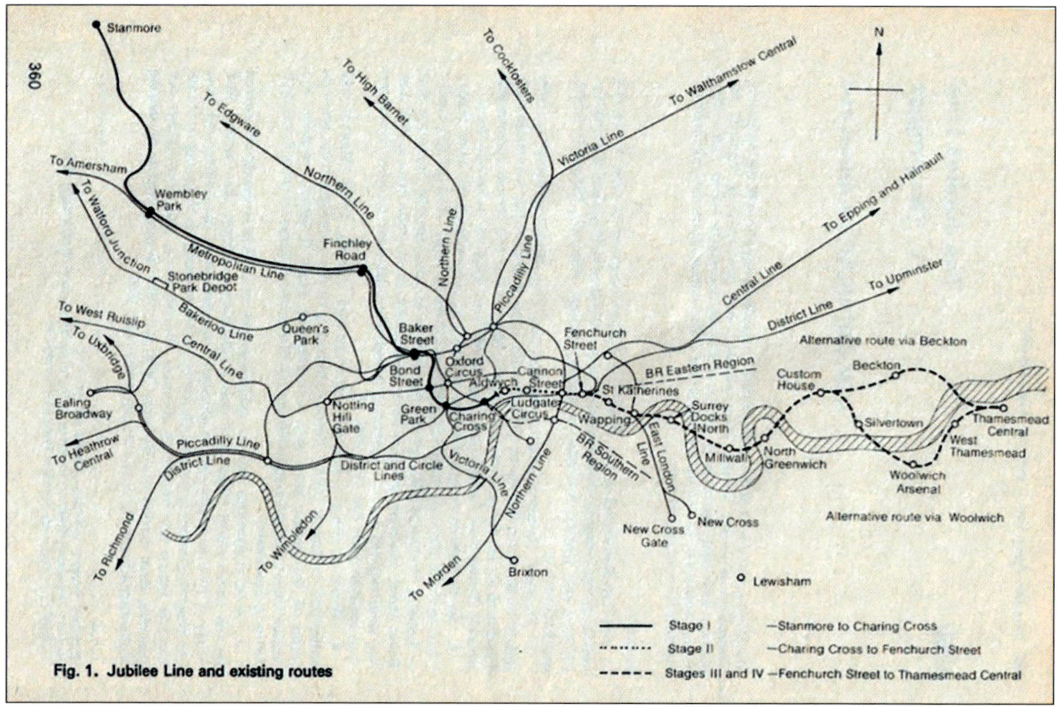

A map produced for a report by the Institute of Civil Engineers in 1979, showing alternative routes to Thamesmead Central via either Beckton or Woolwich Arsenal.

This plan dates from November 1976 and shows the southern route via Woolwich Arsenal (highlighted green), and the alternative route via Beckton (highlighted yellow), including a station at Beckton. The station on the far-right hand side of the plan shows the proposed location of Thamesmead Central station. (Copyright TfL from the TfL Engineering Records Collection)

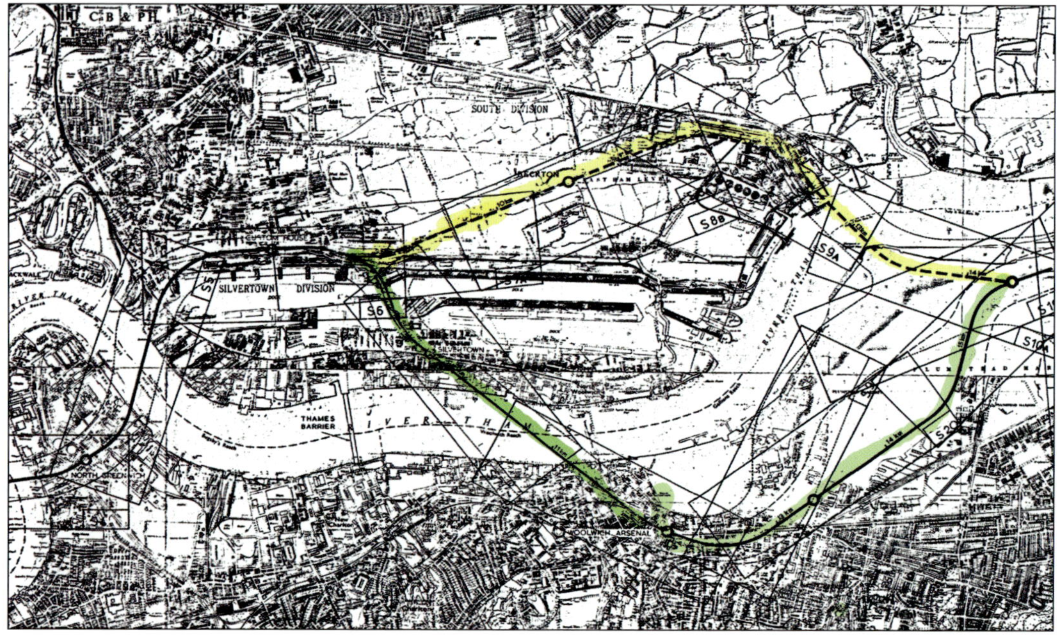

St Katharine's

The station at St Katharine's (also referred to as St Katharine's Dock) would have been located just east of St Katharine's Dock. It would have had three escalators, with the ticket hall facing East Smithfield.

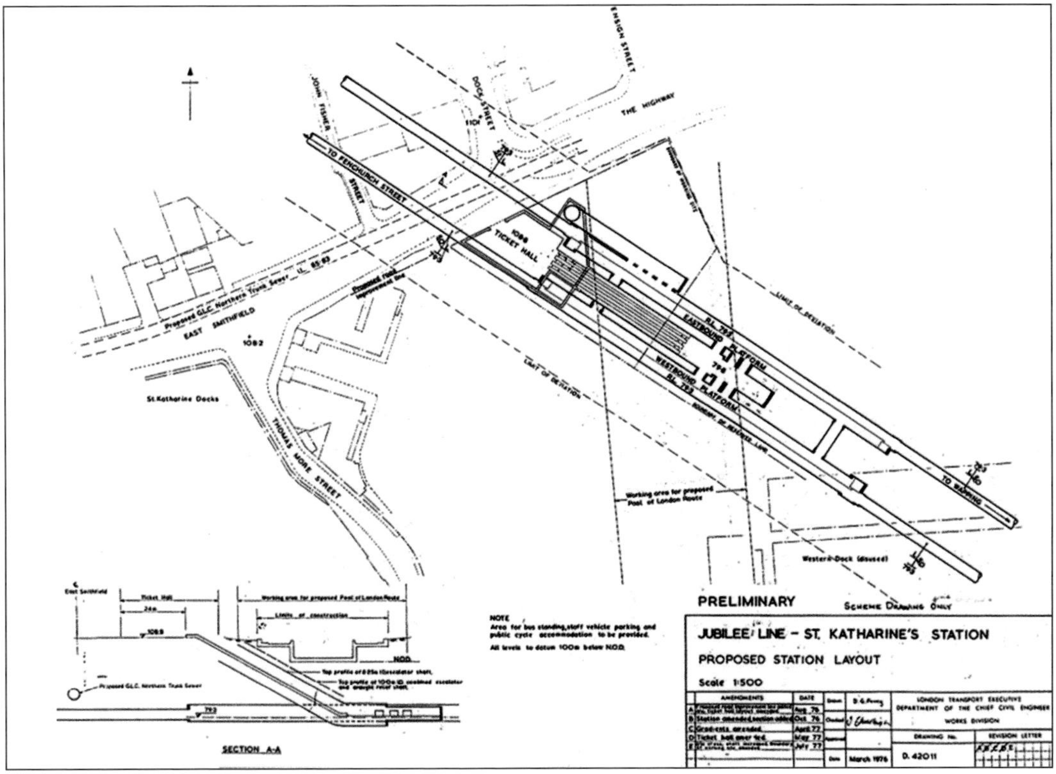

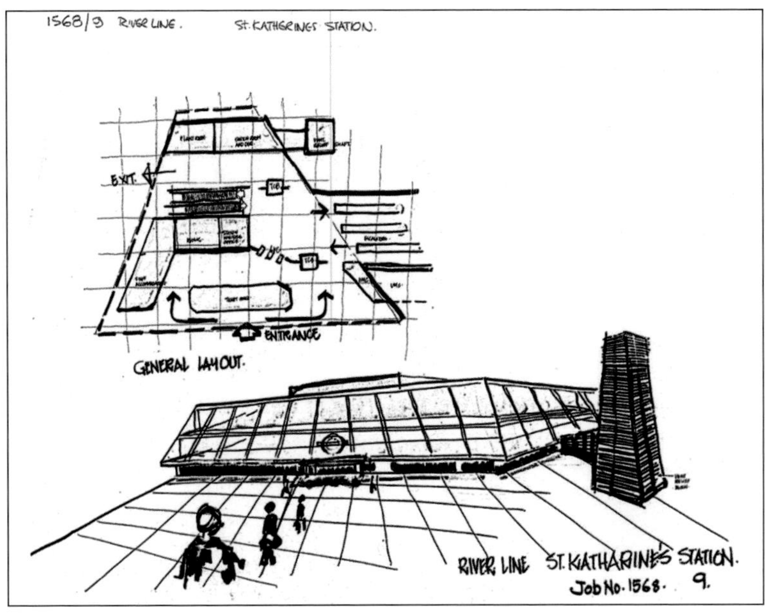

Above: This plan dates from 1977, including several modifications from the original drawing produced in 1976. (Copyright TfL from the TfL Engineering Records Collection)

Right: This is an artist's impression of the proposed station at St Katharine's. The station would have been located to the east of St Katharine's Dock, which has since developed into a vibrant housing and leisure area, with thriving nightlife and a marina. (Copyright TfL from the TfL Engineering Records Collection)

An artist's impression of St Katharine's station. (Karen Baker)

The 1974 London Rail Study (*The Barran Report*) considered two routes, the original Fleet line to New Cross Gate, Lewisham, Addiscombe and Hayes and a second route, referred to as the River line, to serve the Isle of Dogs and Thamesmead. Plans were drawn up for a junction, called St Katharine's Junction, where the two routes would have diverged.

St Katharine's Junction

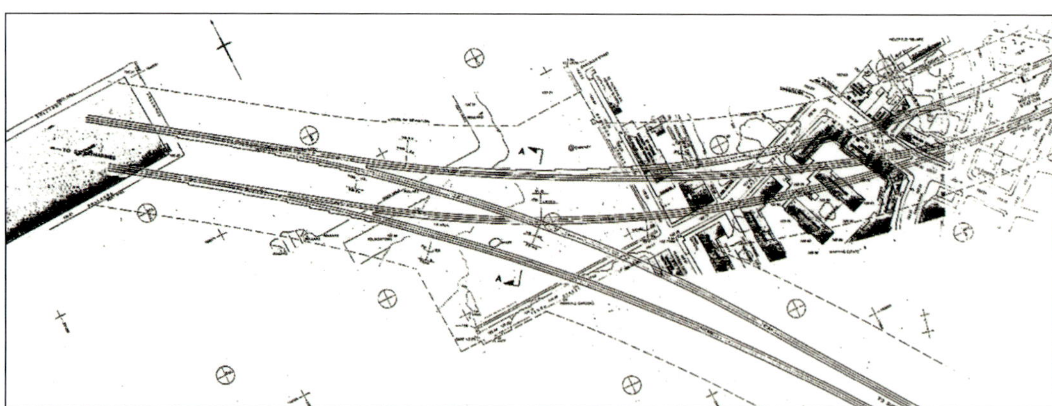

This drawing shows the proposed St Katharine's Junction, with the Fleet line heading towards Lewisham (lower branch) and the River line (often referred to as the Fleet line) towards Thamesmead (top branch). Wapping station is shown in the top right-hand corner of the drawing. As can be seen, planners were undecided on whether to progress with the Lewisham route or the River line alignment towards Thamesmead, or both routes, diverging at St Katharine's Junction. (Copyright TfL from the TfL Engineering Records Collection)

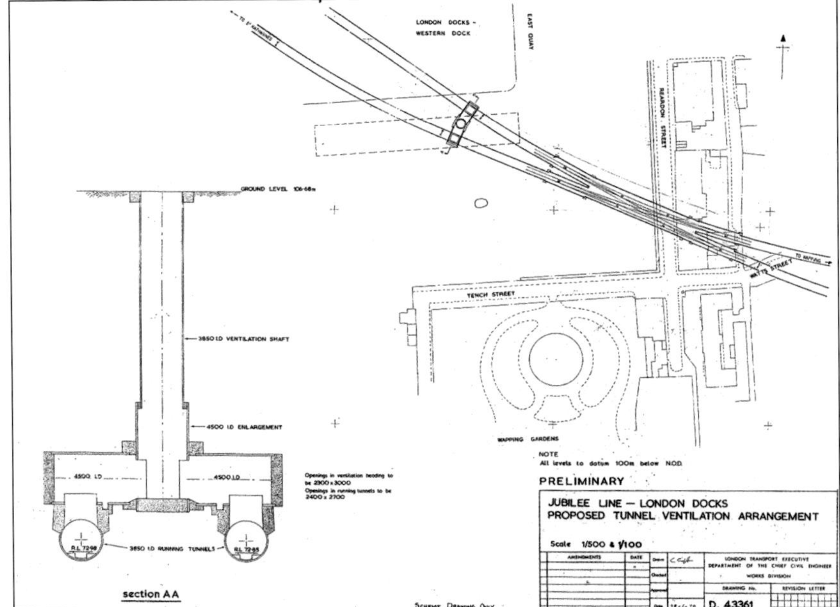

This drawing shows the proposed ventilation shaft and crossovers between St. Katharine's and Wapping. (Copyright TfL from the TfL Engineering Records Collection)

Wapping

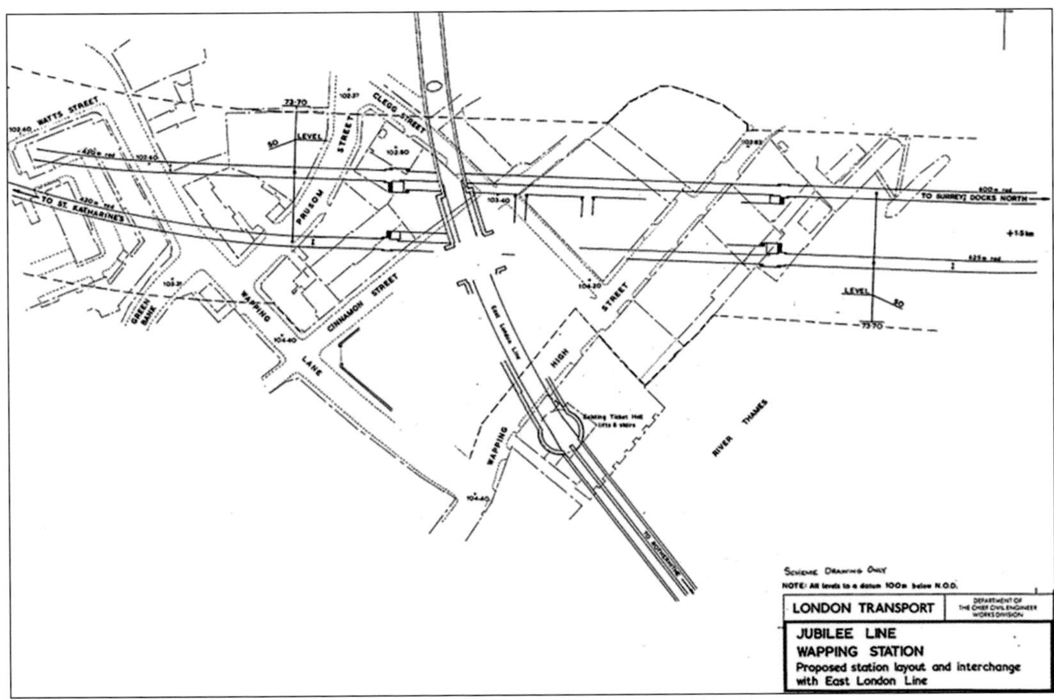

This drawing dates from July 1978 and shows the planned interchange between the Jubilee line and the East London line at Wapping. The Jubilee line runs left to right, with the East London line running north to south. (Copyright TfL from the TfL Engineering Records Collection)

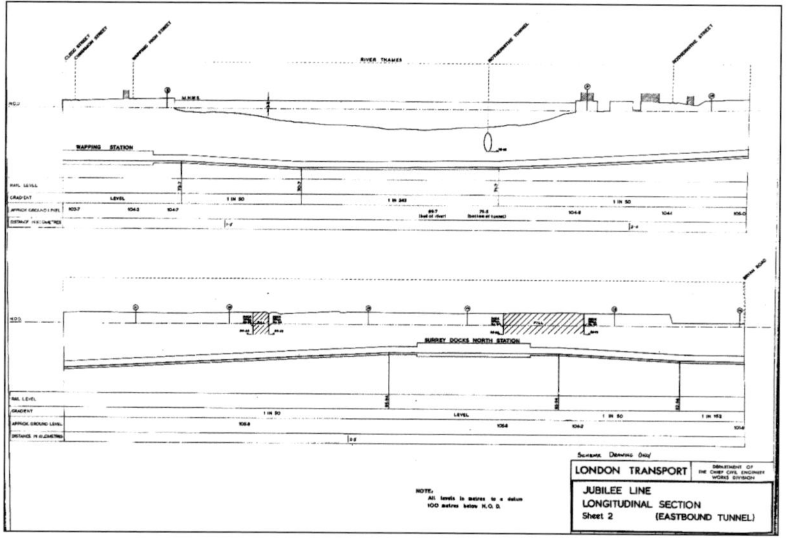

This plan shows the Jubilee line passing beneath the River Thames between Wapping and Surrey Docks North. The Rotherhithe Tunnel is also marked on the plan. As is commonplace on the London Underground, stations are usually constructed on a hill. This provides a small incline to help trains slow down when approaching stations, and a downward gradient to assist with acceleration when leaving. (Copyright TfL from the TfL Engineering Records Collection)

Surrey Docks North

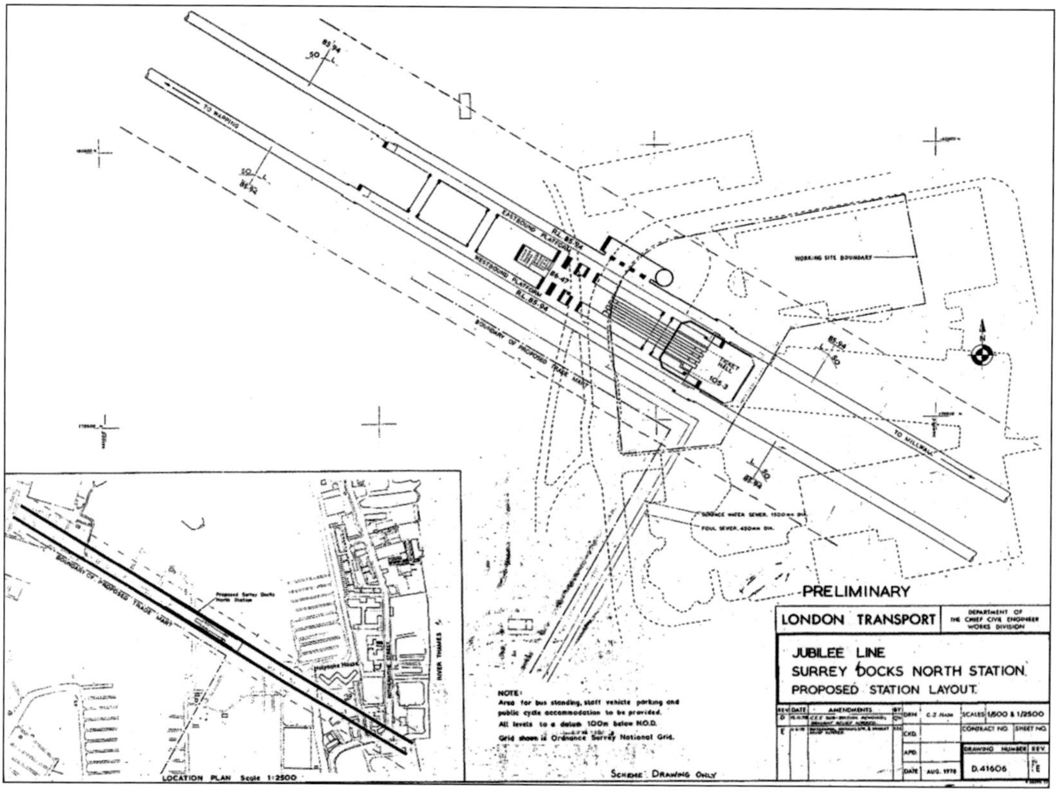

This drawing shows Surrey Docks North station, which would have been located alongside Surrey Basin, just under half a mile from Rotherhithe East London line station. (Copyright TfL from the TfL Engineering Records Collection)

Millwall

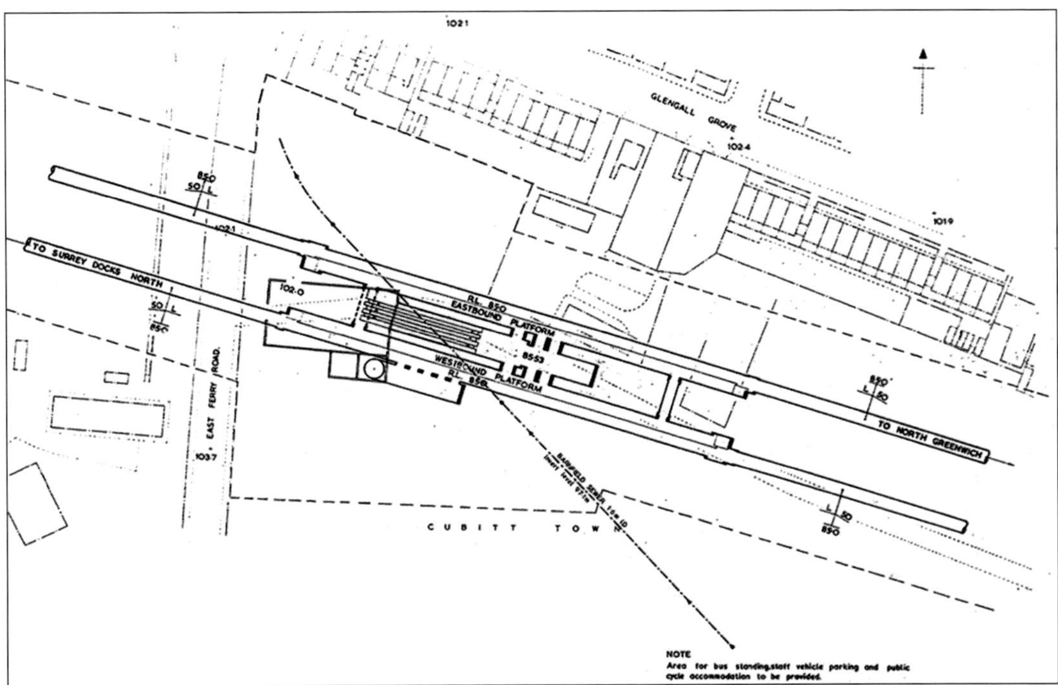

Millwall station, on the Isle of Dogs, would have been located close to the present-day Docklands Light Railway (DLR) station at Crossharbour. As with most of the other stations on the line, the station would have had three escalators leading to the platforms. This plan is dated May 1975. (Copyright TfL from the TfL Engineering Records Collection)

An artist's impression of the proposed station building at Millwall. (Copyright TfL from the TfL Engineering Records Collection)

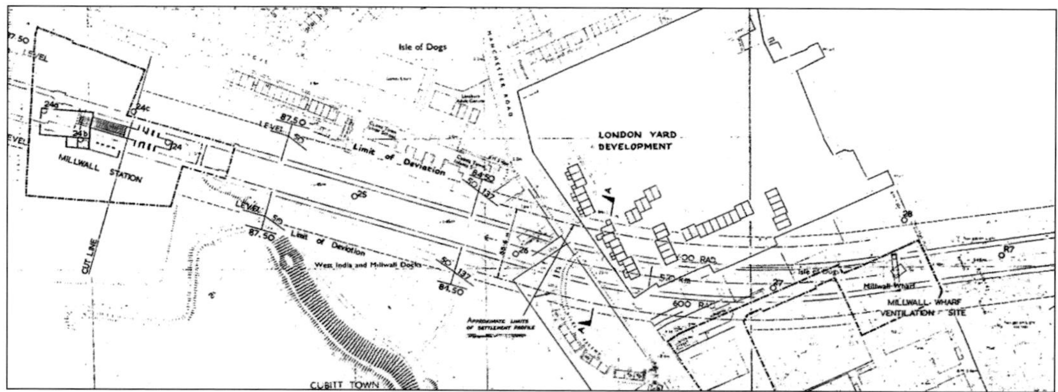

Millwall station is shown on the left of this plan, along with the planned Millwall Wharf ventilation shaft, located to the right of the drawing, shortly before the line passed under the River Thames to North Greenwich. (Copyright TfL from the TfL Engineering Records Collection)

North Greenwich

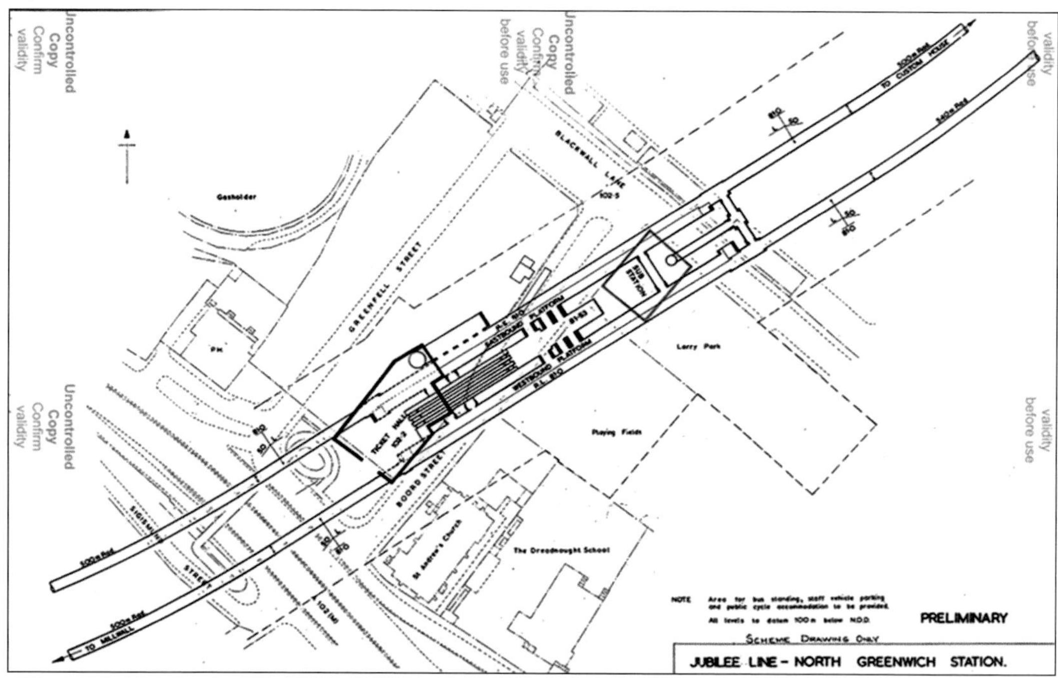

North Greenwich station would have been located below Boord Street, about half a mile south of the current North Greenwich station. The area has changed significantly since this plan was produced in June 1976. St Andrew's Church, located adjacent to the putative station entrance, was demolished in the late 1980s and many of the other roads and buildings have either disappeared or been renamed. (Copyright TfL from the TfL Engineering Records Collection)

Custom House

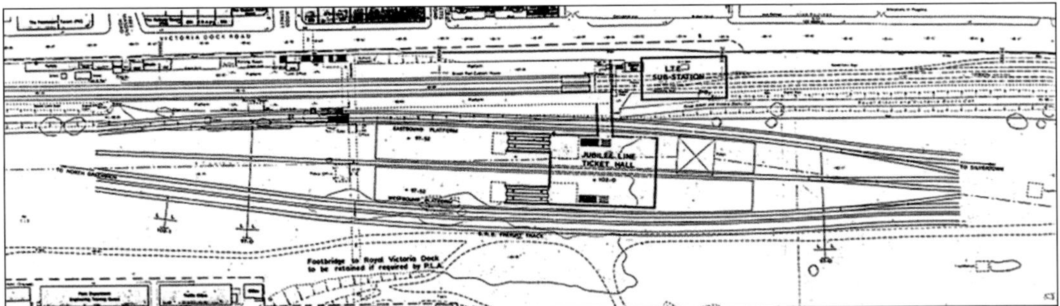

In this plan dated September 1978, Custom House would have been located on the surface, parallel with Victoria Dock Road, and almost on the site of the current Elizabeth line station. The adjacent British Rail line would have been retained and an interchange provided. The British Rail platforms would have been located between the Jubilee line station and Victoria Dock Road. A British Rail freight line would also have been retained to the south of the station, while the Jubilee line station would have been provided with three tracks and two island platforms. Initially, a new depot would have been provided at Custom House, but later plans envisaged it in Beckton instead. Just east of the station, the line would have divided, with one branch towards Beckton and Beckton Depot, and the other continuing towards Silvertown and Woolwich. (Copyright TfL from the TfL Engineering Records Collection)

This is a more detailed plan showing the layout of the station building, which would have been located above the tracks. The central platform would have been reversible, enabling trains to terminate here and run to and from the depot. (Copyright TfL from the TfL Engineering Records Collection)

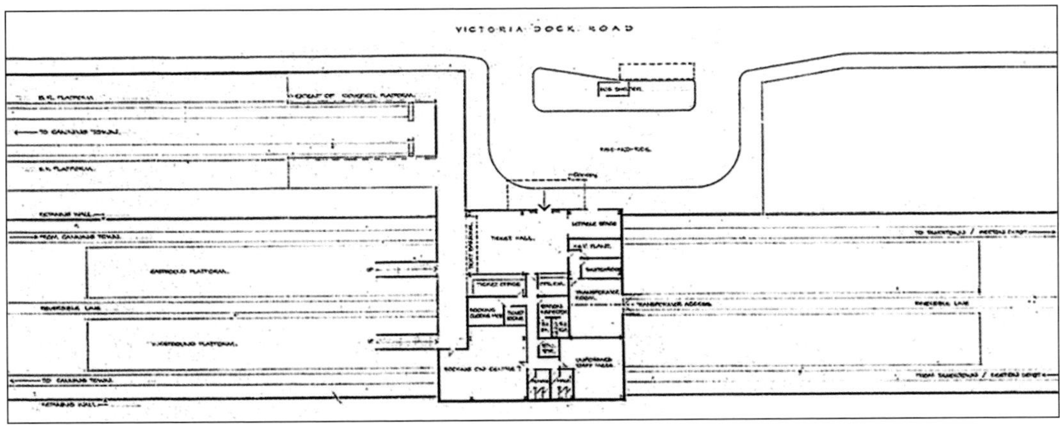

Silvertown

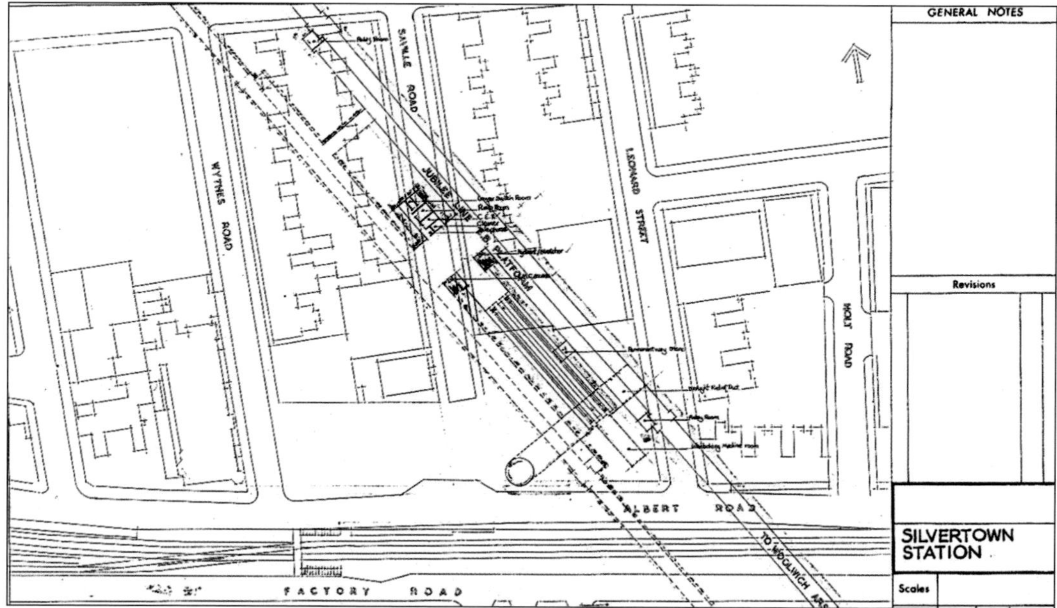

The Jubilee line station at Silvertown would have been just south of the present-day London City Airport DLR station. The tunnels would have passed below the British Rail North Woolwich branch, which runs from left to right across the bottom of the drawing. This alignment is now used by the Elizabeth line. (Copyright TfL from the TfL Engineering Records Collection)

This plan dates from July 1979 and shows the proposed station layout at Silvertown, including three banks of escalators. The site is now used for housing. (Copyright TfL from the TfL Engineering Records Collection)

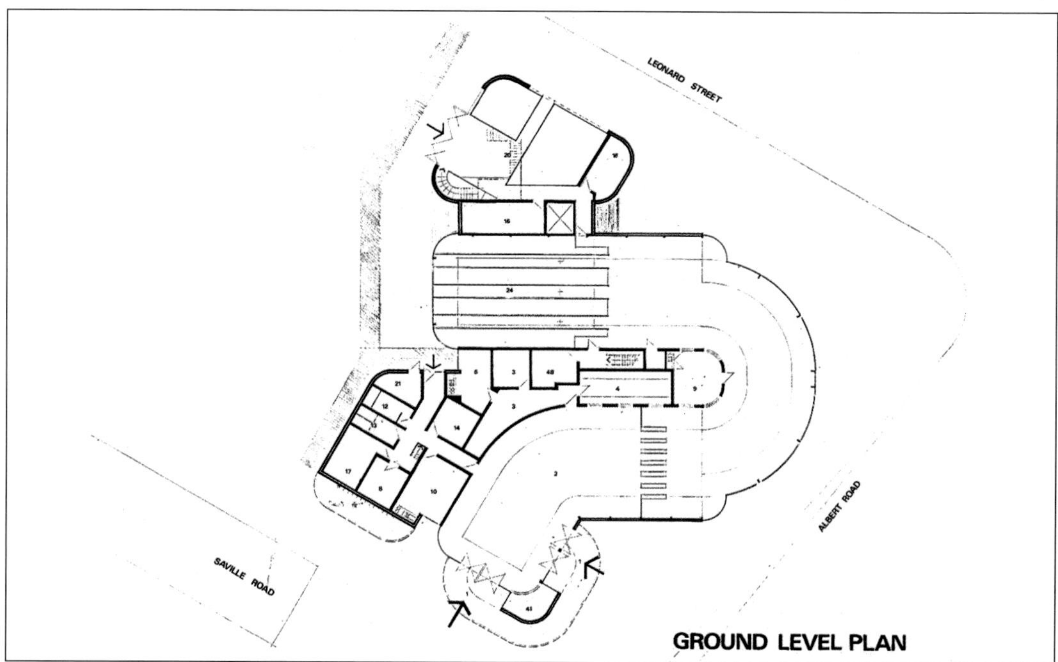

Woolwich Arsenal

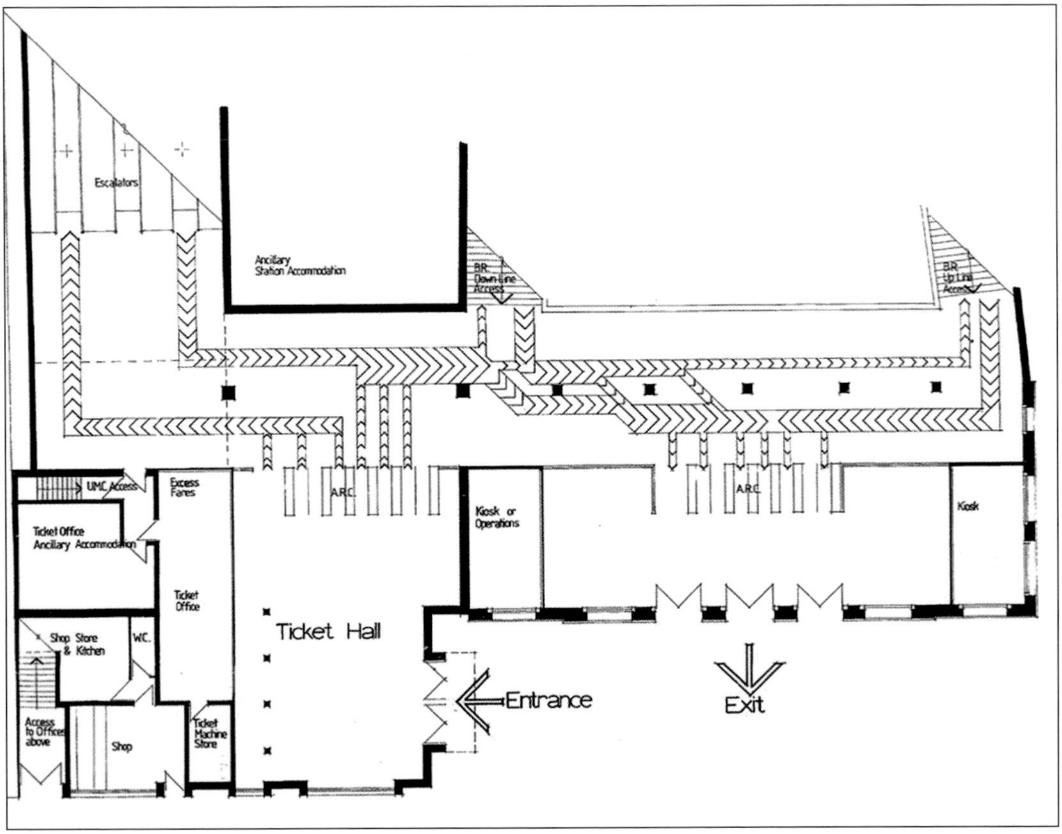

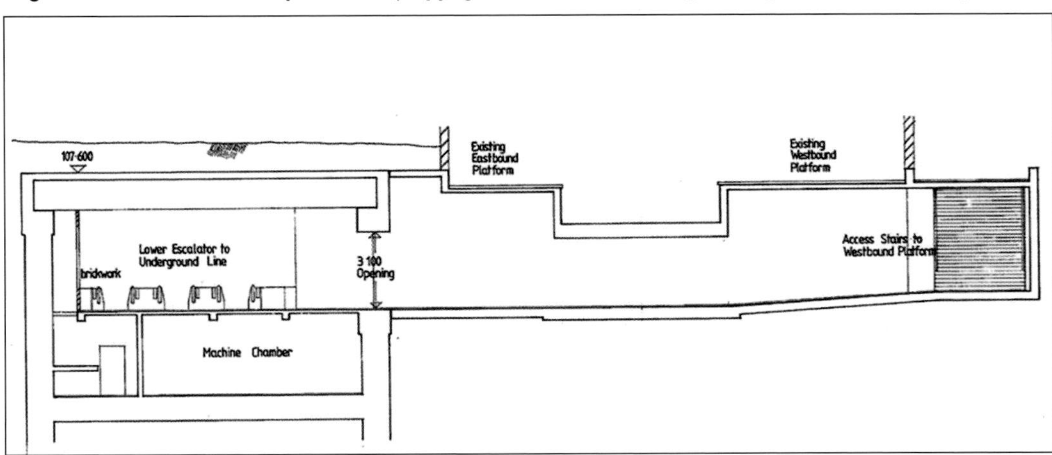

The above plan, produced in January 1979, shows the proposed station layout, with arrows showing the main passenger flows. At top right of the drawing are the existing main-line platforms at Woolwich Arsenal, which are now used by Southeastern and Thameslink services. (Copyright TfL from the TfL Engineering Records Collection)

This plan, drawn in August 1979, shows the connection from the main line platforms to the Jubilee line booking hall and escalators. The Jubilee line platforms would have been located underground on a parallel alignment with the main-line platforms. (Copyright TfL from the TfL Engineering Records Collection)

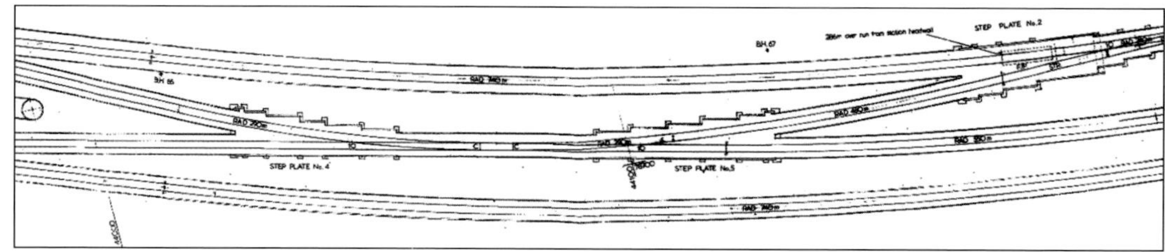

To the east of Woolwich Arsenal there would have been a crossover line and a turnback siding located between the two running tunnels. The reversing siding is the middle tunnel located on the right-hand side of the plan, with Woolwich Arsenal station to the left. (Copyright TfL from the TfL Engineering Records Collection)

Woolwich Arsenal–Thamesmead

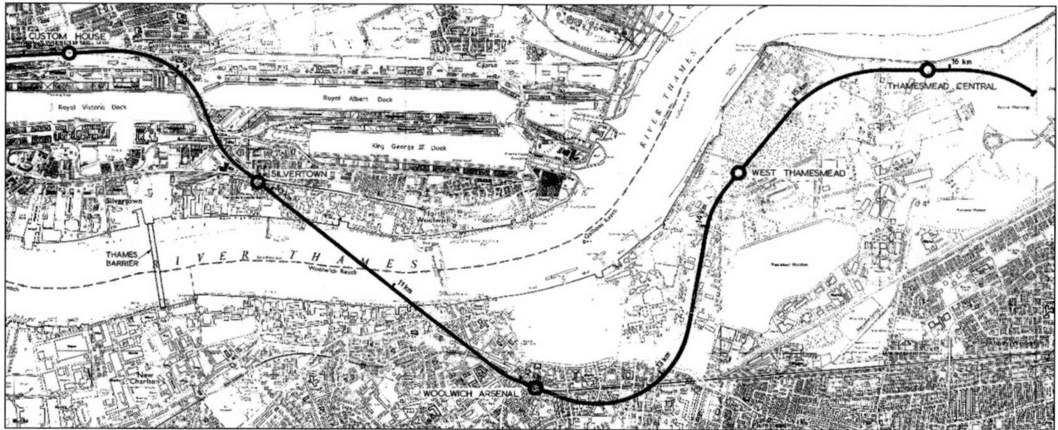

The above plan shows the planned route between Custom House and Thamesmead Central via Woolwich Arsenal. (Copyright TfL from the TfL Engineering Records Collection)

West Thamesmead

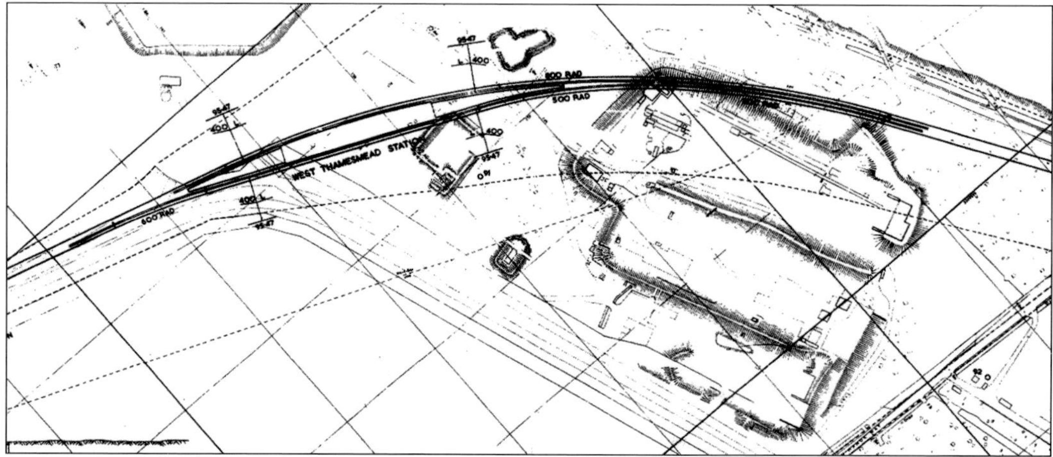

The approach to West Thamesmead would have utilised 'cut-and-cover' tunnels, rather than the deep level bored tunnels used elsewhere on the proposed line. (Copyright TfL from the TfL Engineering Records Collection)

Thamesmead Central

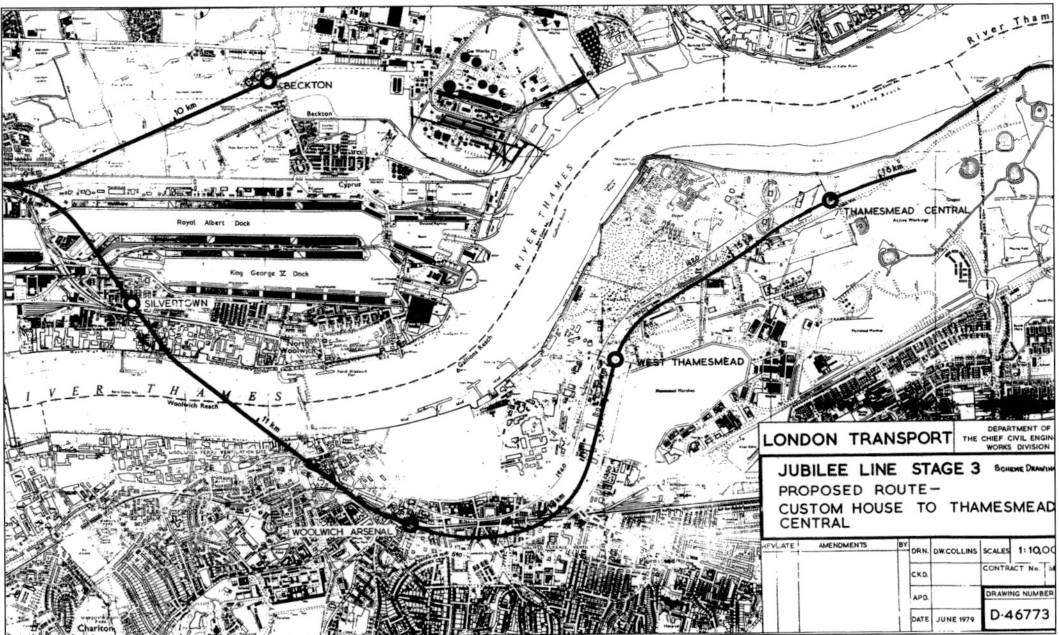

The above plan shows a revised plan of the route between Custom House and Thamesmead Central, including the proposed branch to Beckton. (Copyright TfL from the TfL Engineering Records Collection)

Beckton

In 1977/78, options were developed for a branch from Custom House to Beckton, where a depot would have been constructed. Two options were considered, one with Beckton on a through line from Custom House to Thamesmead and the other with Beckton as a terminus.

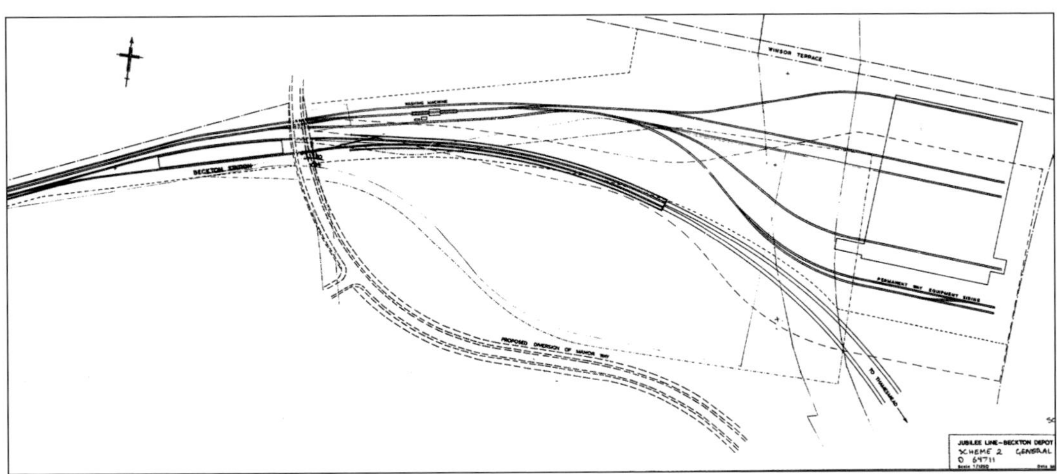

The above plan shows the proposed Beckton station on the left-hand side, with a branch to the depot and the main line continuing to Thamesmead. (Copyright TfL from the TfL Engineering Records Collection)

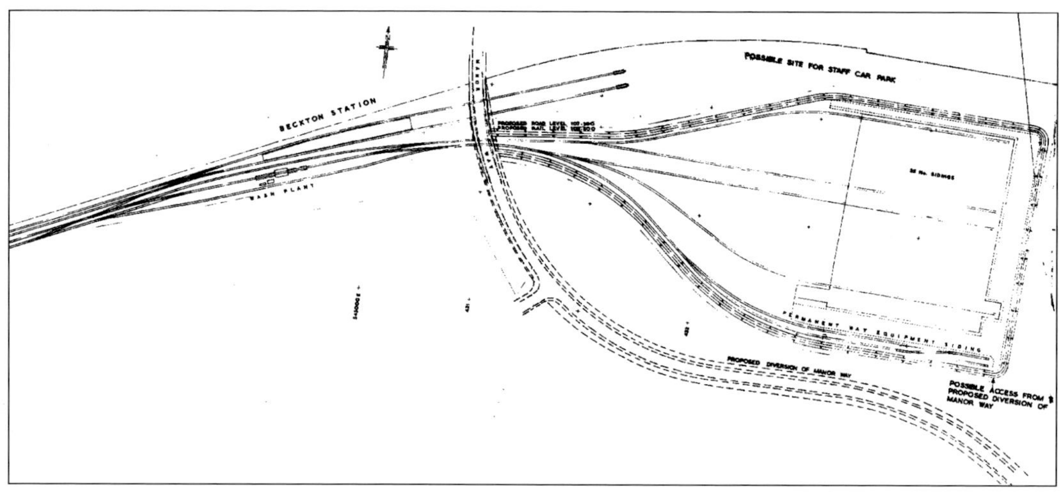

This plan shows Beckton station as a terminus, with a separate branch serving Beckton Depot. (Copyright TfL from the TfL Engineering Records Collection)

An Interim Solution

The planning consent for the Fleet line included provision for one of the tunnels between Custom House and Woolwich to be built to main-line gauge.

Plans were drawn up for diverting the British Rail North Woolwich branch to Woolwich Arsenal, utilising a single main-line gauge tunnel. A temporary connection to the British Rail North Woolwich branch would have been constructed at Custom House, with an interim station constructed at Silvertown; this would have a single platform but with provision for a second.

Initially, only a single platform would have been built at Woolwich Arsenal, with provision for the second platform and cross-passages to be constructed at a later date. Consideration was also given to a further extension to Plumstead, enabling services from Custom House to join the North Kent line and enabling passenger and freight services to continue towards Dartford.

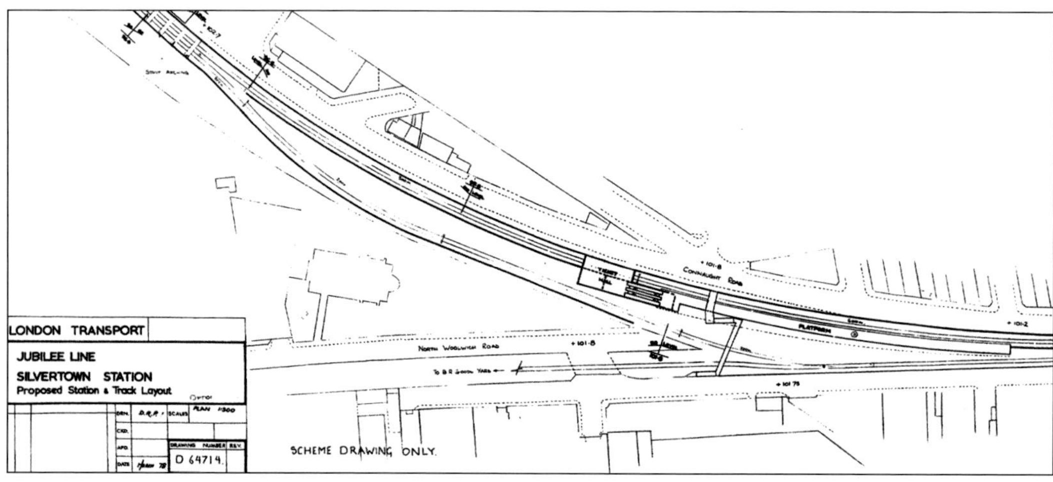

This drawing was produced in March 1978 and shows the interim proposals for Silvertown, with a single track and platform and connections to the freight siding. (Copyright TfL from the TfL Engineering Records Collection)

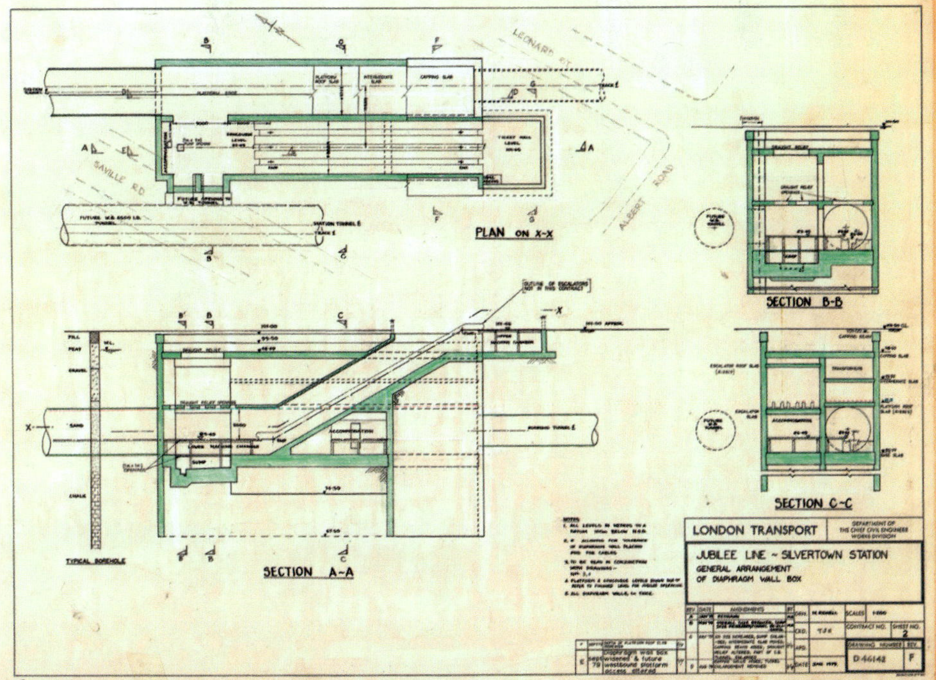

This drawing, dating from 1979, shows the interim arrangements at Silvertown. (Copyright TfL from the TfL Engineering Records Collection)

This drawing was produced in April 1978 and shows the cross-section of the tunnels (top) and a plan view of the platform at Woolwich Arsenal (bottom). The lower tunnel, shown with dotted lines, is the site of the second (westbound) platform, which would have been built at a later date. (Copyright TfL from the TfL Engineering Records Collection)

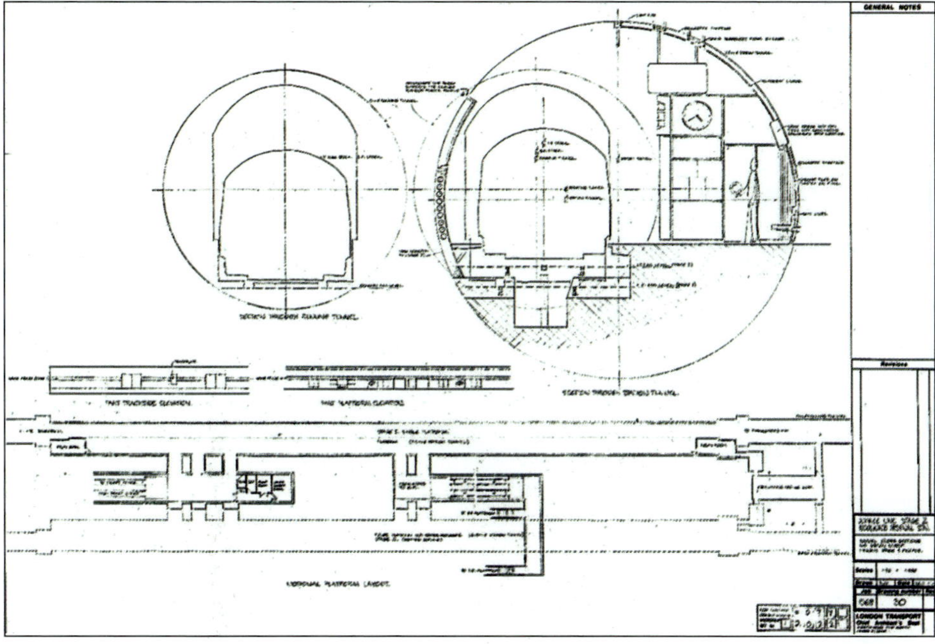

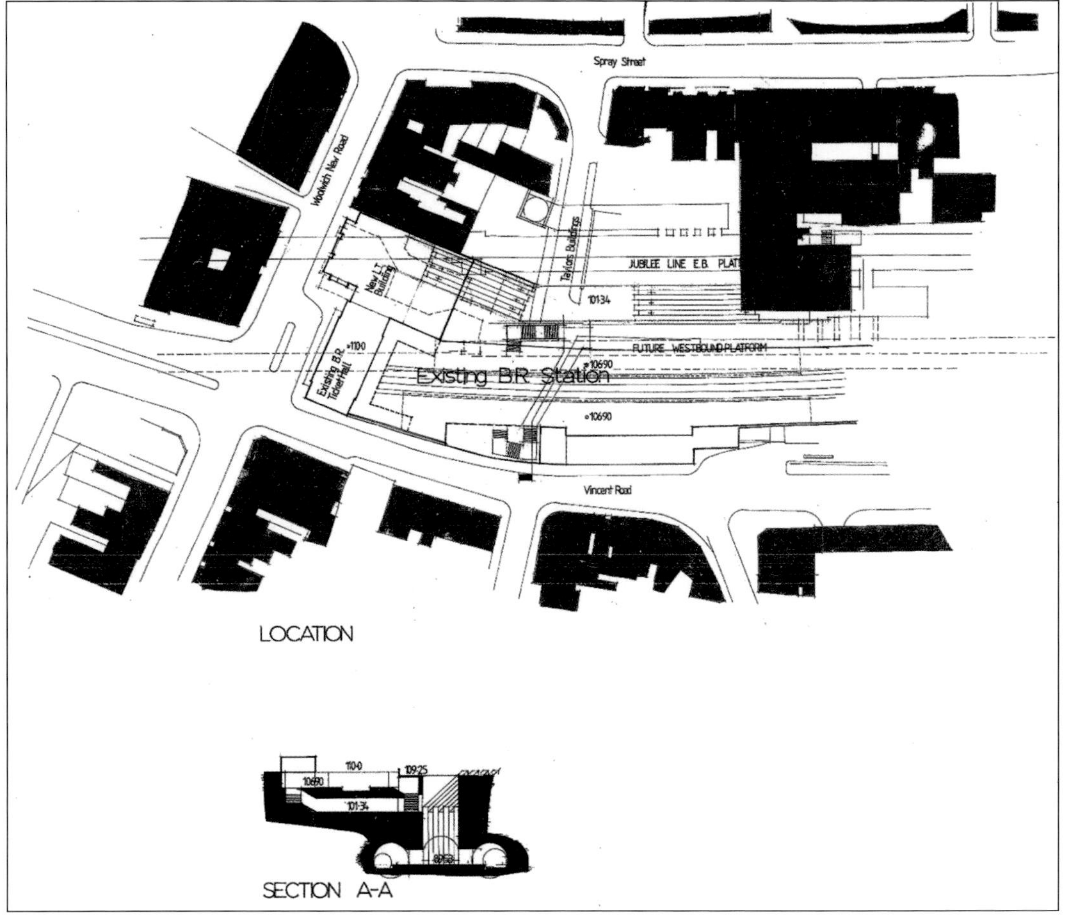

This is a plan of the interim arrangements proposed at Woolwich Arsenal. The existing British Rail station is shown, with the Jubilee line ticket hall added to the north side of the existing booking hall. Escalators then lead down to the platform. The eastbound Jubilee line platform is shown, with dotted lines indicating where the future eastbound platform would be located. (Copyright TfL from the TfL Engineering Records Collection)

1980 Proposals

London Transport eventually secured planning consent for the section between Fenchurch Street and Woolwich Arsenal in August 1980. It was assumed that a branch would be constructed to a depot at Beckton, but land issues prevented this section from being included in the legislation.

An alternative option was drawn up in 1980 for a Thamesmead loop, which would have been constructed as a light rail scheme with an interchange with the Jubilee line station at Thamesmead. The light rail line would have commenced at Custom House, with stations at West Beckton, Beckton, West Thamesmead and Thamesmead Central. Additional stations may have been provided at Gallions Reach and South Thamesmead, with a small depot at Beckton.

Another proposal was for a route serving Fenchurch Street, Wapping, Surrey Docks, Isle of Dogs, North Greenwich and Custom House, after which the line would have divided, with one branch to Thamesmead via Beckton and a second route via Silvertown, Royal Docks and Woolwich Arsenal to Thamesmead.

1980 also saw the publication of a joint report produced by the Department of the Environment, the Greater London Council, the Docklands Development Corporation and London Transport, which considered

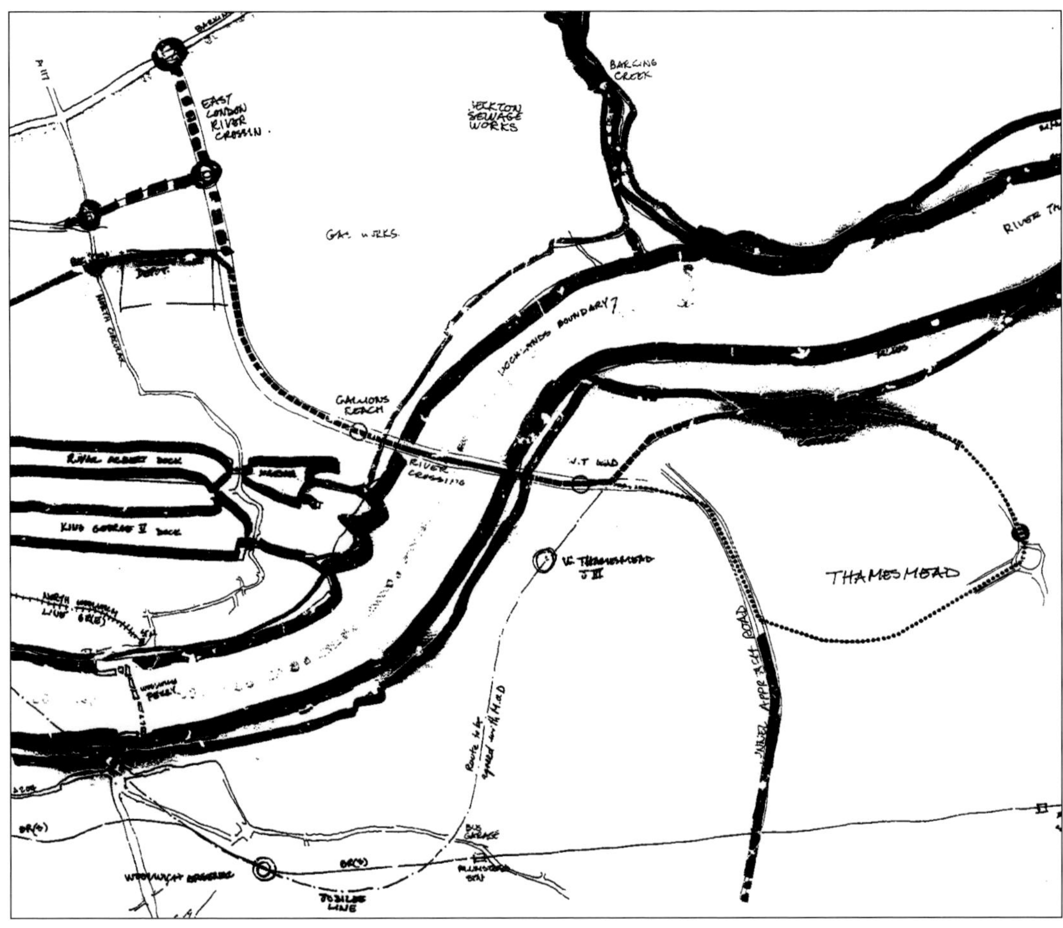

This drawing shows the Jubilee line, towards the bottom of the drawing, terminating at Thamesmead. A light rail route would have utilised the proposed East London River Crossing to connect Custom House and Thamesmead, with a loop service two or three stations in Thamesmead. (Copyright TfL from the TfL Engineering Records Collection)

cheaper transport alternatives for London's docklands. This included a Jubilee line extension from Charing Cross to Beckton via Cannon Street and Fenchurch Street with no branch to Thamesmead. Other options included express busways, a light railway between Aldgate East and Beckton / North Greenwich or a tram between Aldgate East and Beckton.

1981 Reports

London Transport revisited the options in its *1981 Annual Report*, which considered a new branch of the East London line from Rotherhithe to the Isle of Dogs and Millwall or a branch from Wapping to Tower Hill.

The London Docklands Development Committee (LDDC) also commenced a study in 1981 to look at transport links to the London docklands. In 1982, The Docklands Public Transport and Access Steering Group published a report concerning transport provision in this area. All these reports looked at express bus services, extending the East London line to the Isle of Dogs, extending the Jubilee line or providing a light rail system from Mile End or the City to the Isle of Dogs. The recommendation was to progress with a light rail system, which was the genesis of the Docklands Light Railway (DLR).

The 1985 Proposal

The Greater London Council (GLC) took one final look at extending the Jubilee line, publishing a report in 1985 called *Public Transport – The Next Ten Years*. The report suggested an extension of the Jubilee line from Charing Cross to Thamesmead via London Bridge, Greenwich, Woolwich and Abbey Wood, utilising the existing British Rail North Kent line for much of the route. The same report also proposed several possible extensions to the DLR, which was under construction at the time.

The 1987 Proposal

In 1987, London Regional Transport (LRT), as was now the identity of the capital's transport organisation, announced that it was considering an extension of the Jubilee line from Charing Cross to London Bridge via Blackfriars and possibly beyond. The *London Daily News* reported that the proposal would include an additional stop on the Waterloo and City line at Blackfriars and would head onwards to Camberwell and Peckham, resurrecting a previous Bakerloo line extension proposal.

The Railways for London Report

The Campaign to Improve London's Transport (CILT) research and resources unit published a report called *Railways for London – Investment Proposals for the LRT Tube and BR Network*, based on a report by Peter Kay.

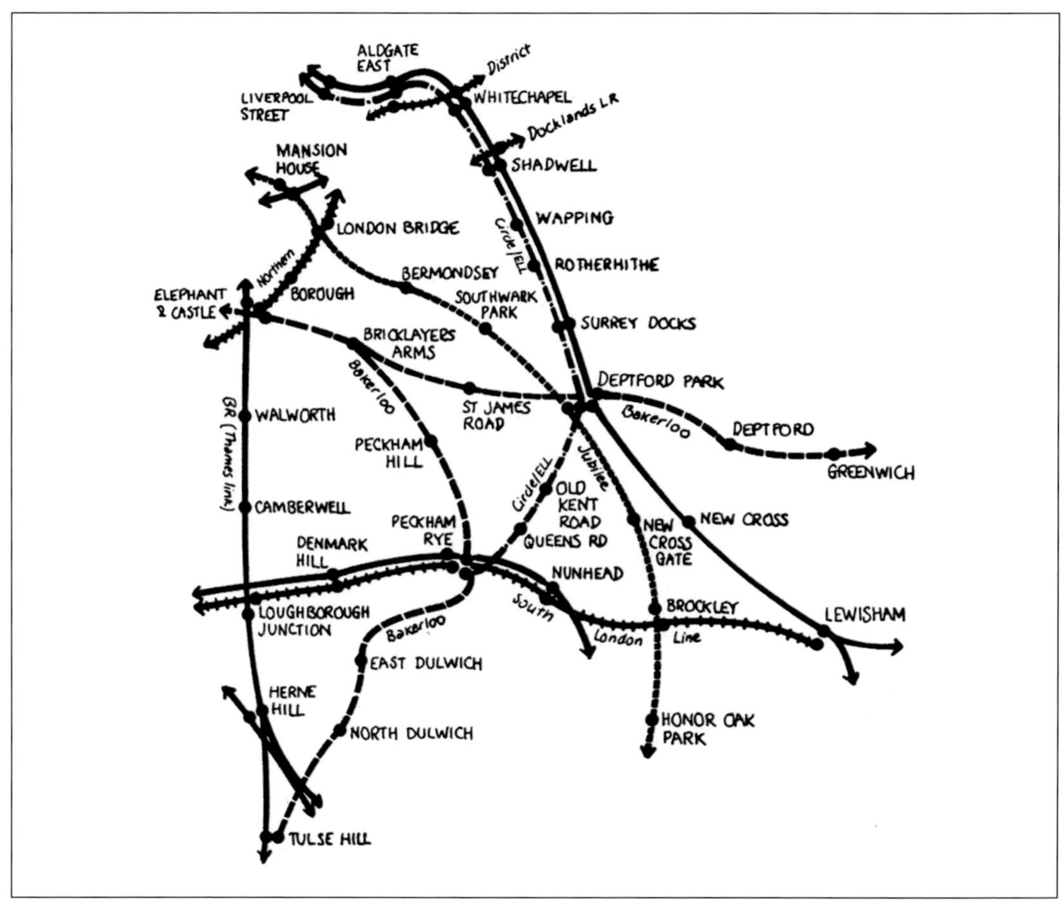

A map from the *Railways for London Report*, which proposed an extension of the Jubilee line to West Croydon via New Cross Gate.

The report recommended extending the Jubilee line from Charing Cross to West Croydon via Aldwych, Blackfriars, Monument, London Bridge, Bermondsey (two stations), Southwark Park, Deptford Park and New Cross Gate, after which trains would surface and join the existing British Rail network, calling at all stations to West Croydon, with a possible branch to Crystal Palace (similar to the recent London Overground extension). The proposal would be combined with several other rail schemes, and was estimated to cost £300 million (excluding rolling stock).

The report also proposed an extension of the Bakerloo line from Elephant & Castle to Bricklayers Arms, where the route would divide, with one branch running to Tulse Hill via Peckham and Dulwich and the other branch extending to Deptford, Plumstead and Abbey Wood or Thamesmead.

It was also suggested that the Jubilee line could serve Abbey Wood and/or West Croydon, leaving the Bakerloo line to serve Peckham and Tulse Hill.

River Line Planning Consent

River Line Stage	Planning Approval Obtained
Fenchurch Street–Woolwich Arsenal	1 August 1980
Custom House–Beckton	Not secured due to unresolved land ownership issues
Woolwich Arsenal–Thamesmead	Not progressed

Proposed signal cabin and relay room codes

Location	Proposed Code
Stanmore	MK (existing code retained)
Baker Street	BM (existing code retained)
Charing Cross	TG
Fenchurch Street	TH
Spare	TJ
Surrey Docks	TL
New Cross	TM
New Cross Gate	TN
Lewisham	TS
Spares	TA, TE, TF, TT, TU, TW, TY, TZ
Custom House	Not allocated
Custom House Depot	Not allocated
Thamesmead Central	Not allocated

Chapter 6

The Jubilee Line Extension (JLE)

The London Docklands Development Corporation (LDDC) was established in 1981 to oversee the redevelopment of the London docklands.

Following the cancellation of Jubilee line Stages 2, 3 and 4 and the River line, a number of other options were considered. Funding constraints resulted in the lower-cost Docklands Light Railway (DLR) being constructed.

Canary Wharf Rail Proposals

The Docklands Light Railway opened in August 1987 and was a catalyst for the redevelopment of London's docklands that has continued to this day.

It soon became clear, however, that the developments around Canary Wharf on the Isle of Dogs would need enhanced transport links. Some improvements were made to the initial DLR network, including an extension to Bank, but these were still not sufficient.

In 1988, the main developer Olympia and York put forward proposals for an extension of the Bakerloo line from Waterloo to Canary Wharf via London Bridge or Bricklayers Arms, with two branches; one from Canary Wharf towards Stratford (or Tottenham Hale) and the other towards the Royal Docks. An extension beyond Elephant & Castle to connect with the existing Bakerloo line was also considered.

Olympia and York then set to work developing its own privately funded underground railway scheme. This would have been known as the Waterloo and Greenwich Railway, operating four- or five-carriage trains between Waterloo and Westcombe Park via Southwark, London Bridge, Surrey Quays, Isle of Dogs (Canary Wharf), Blackwall Point (North Greenwich) and Greenwich Parkway. It was also sometimes referred to as the CanaryLoo line.

The Waterloo and Greenwich Railway's depot would have been located at Westcombe Park. Two branches were considered, one from Blackwall Point to Stratford and the other from Greenwich Parkway to Woolwich Arsenal and Thamesmead. Also envisaged was a further extension towards Paddington.

The Central London Rail Study

Paul Channon became Secretary of State for Transport in 1987 and commissioned the *Central London Rail Study* in March 1988. The study, published in January 1989, was conducted by the Department of Transport, British Rail, London Regional Transport and London Underground, and examined several rail options.

Two primary options for extending the Jubilee line were as follows:

- Charing Cross to Whitechapel via Aldwych (the Piccadilly line station was still open at this time), Ludgate/Blackfriars, St Paul's and Liverpool Street, with the principal aim of relieving overcrowding on the Central line.
- Charing Cross to London Bridge via Ludgate/Blackfriars. This would have facilitated a further extension into the London docklands and was offered as an alternative to the Olympia and York scheme.

Three further extensions were then examined, as follows:

- Whitechapel to Stratford.
- Stratford to Ilford, with stations near Forest Gate and Manor Park.
- Stratford to Hainault via Leytonstone, sharing Central line tracks as far as Leytonstone, before taking over the Central line branch to Hainault.

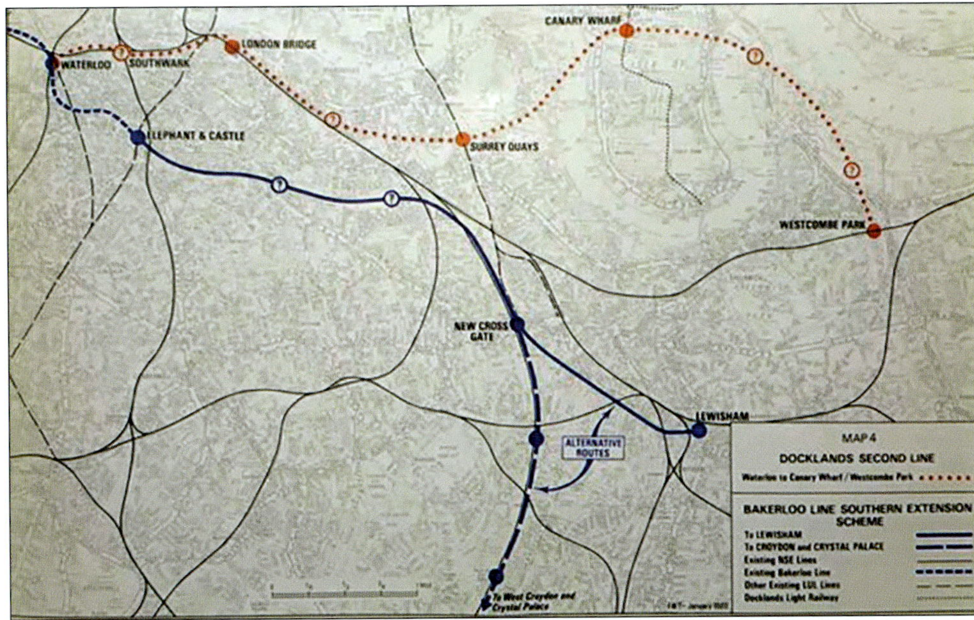

The above plan shows the proposed standalone railway from Waterloo to Westcombe Park via Canary Wharf, which would have been mostly privately funded. In addition, an option for extending the Bakerloo line from Elephant & Castle towards Lewisham, Croydon and Crystal Palace is shown. This is not dissimilar to the current proposals for extending the Bakerloo line to Lewisham. (*Central London Rail Study*)

This plan contains two options for extending the Jubilee line from Charing Cross. Both options would have served Ludgate with one option crossing the river to London Bridge, while the other option envisaged a route via Liverpool Street to Whitechapel. Three further extensions were considered for the route beyond Whitechapel, the first taking the existing line to Stratford. From Stratford, two options were proposed, one to Ilford and the other to Hainault via Leytonstone. (*Central London Rail Study*)

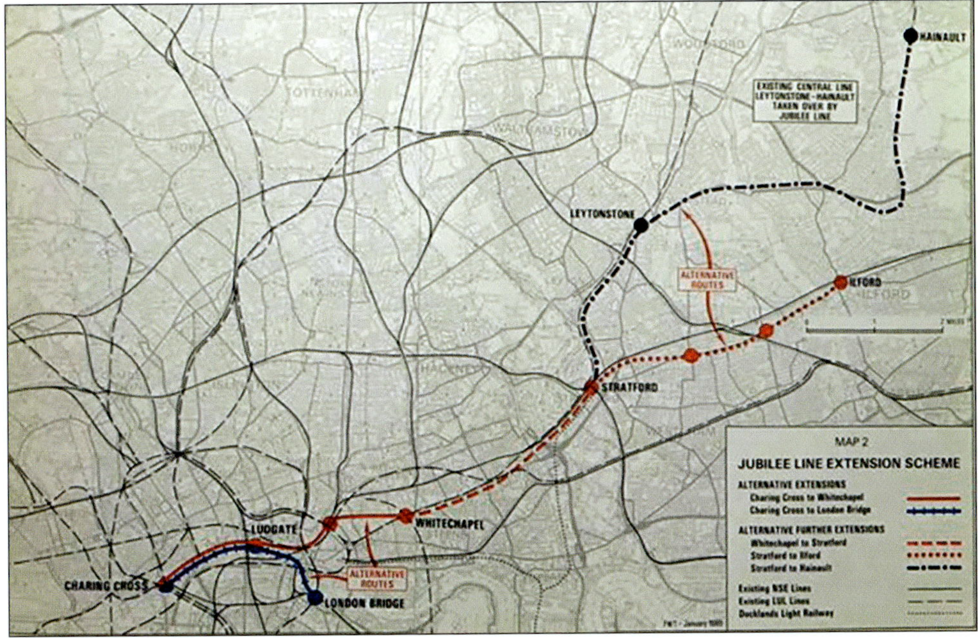

The option with the strongest business case was an extension to Ilford, the estimated cost of which, including rolling stock, was £640 million.

The Olympia and York proposal was also included in the report and was referred to as the Docklands Second Line, with a route from Waterloo to Westcombe Park via Southwark, London Bridge, Surrey Quays and Canary Wharf.

The East London Rail Study

Following publication of the *Central London Rail Study*, a separate *East London Rail Study* was commissioned to look at solutions for meeting transport demands related to the growth of the London docklands.

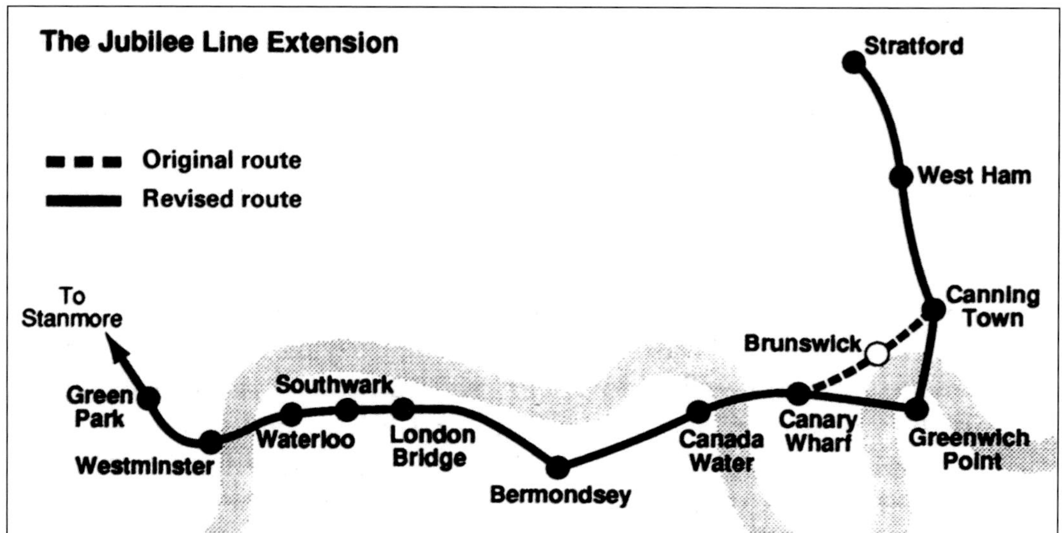

The Jubilee Line Extension was initially intended to serve a new development at Brunswick Wharf, but this was later amended to serve North Greenwich, shown as Greenwich Point on this map. (From *Developing London's Docklands* by Sue Brownhill)

This map shows the options for a future extension towards the Royal Docks and Woolwich Arsenal.

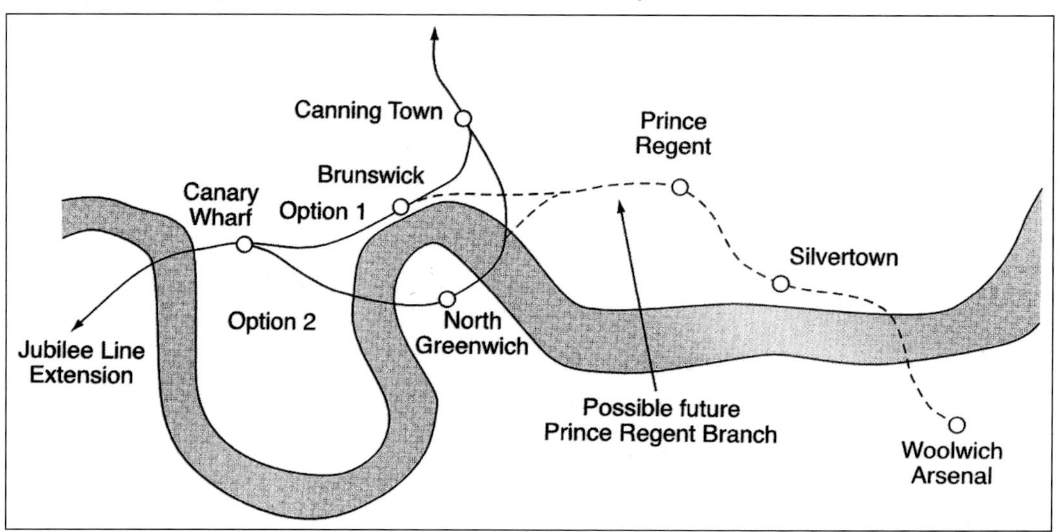

The main purpose of the *East London Rail Study* was to assess options for a new rail link to London Docklands to supplement the Docklands Light Railway. The remit was to evaluate an extension of the Jubilee line alongside the Olympia and York proposal.

By then, Cecil Parkinson was Secretary of State for Transport, and although London Regional Transport preferred a route via Aldwych and Ludgate Circus to London Docklands, the final Jubilee Line Extension (JLE) was routed via Westminster, Waterloo and London Bridge.

A proposed extension via the Royal Docks to Woolwich and Thamesmead was not progressed, although the Jubilee Line Extension included the construction of a junction near North Greenwich, which would facilitate a future branch towards the Royal Docks.

Approval

The 16km (9.93-mile) Jubilee Line Extension project finally received approval, including a private-sector funding contribution from Olympia and York.

Station Design and Architecture

The design of the stations was overseen by Roland Paoletti and the Jubilee Line Extension architect's office. Paoletti was previously the Chief Architect of the Hong Kong Mass Transit Railway (MTR), where he was involved with the construction of three lines, 36 stations and three depots.

A number of different architects were brought in to design the stations, which incorporated the latest safety features, including platform-edge doors at the underground stations. The JLE was the first railway in London to use these, with the concept later installed on the subsequent Elizabeth line's new underground stations. A number of lessons learnt from the King's Cross station fire of 1987 were incorporated in the station designs. At the time of construction, however, some of the adjacent sites had not been fully developed, so the stations were designed from the outset with additional capacity to facilitate future growth.

Station and Depot Architects

Station	Architect	Comments
Westminster	Michael Hopkins and Partners	2000 Civic Trust Building of the Year
Waterloo	JLE Project Architects	
Southwark	MacCormac Jamieson Prichard	
London Bridge	Weston Williamson / JLE Project Architects	
Bermondsey	Ian Ritchie	
Canada Water	Herron Associates / JLE Project Architects	New bus station designed by Eva Jiricná
Canary Wharf	Foster and Partners	2000 Civic Trust Building of the Year
North Greenwich	Alsop, Lyall and Störmer	New bus station designed by Foster and Partners
Canning Town	Troughton McAslan	
West Ham	Van Heyningen and Haward	
Stratford	Troughton McAslan and Wilkinson Eyre	
Stratford Market Depot	Chris Wilkinson Architects	

The Royal Fine Art Commission named the extension as its Millennium Building of the Year.

A Stratford to North Woolwich train about to pass under the Northern outfall sewer, between Abbey Road and West Ham, in September 1978. This route is now part of the DLR, with the Jubilee line using the underbridge to the left. (Robert Mitchell)

Construction

Detailed plans were made to protect the environment during the construction of the Jubilee Line Extension and the historic finds expected to be uncovered along the route. The project also engaged with local communities and rail passengers to explain the benefits of the project.

Westminster station proved to be a particular challenge due to its proximity to Westminster Bridge, the Houses of Parliament and the Elizabeth Tower (more commonly known as Big Ben). In addition, the new station and booking hall needed to be built around the existing Circle and District line station, which had to remain operational throughout. The station also had to accommodate foundations for the new Portcullis House office building. Original plans to utilise Parliament Square as a construction site were rejected. The solution was to construct a multi-level station located in a 40m-deep box.

Waterloo station was constructed beneath the main line station, with the main entrance accommodated within the station arches and colonnade adjacent to Waterloo Road; this required the removal of several bus stops. Below ground, a travelator was provided, linking the Jubilee line platforms to the Bakerloo and Northern lines.

Southwark station included a connection to Waterloo East station. The circular station entrance building is located opposite TfL's Palestra office building.

London Bridge station has seen radical change over the last 25 years, commencing with the Jubilee Line Extension. Further development has been undertaken as part of the Thameslink Project and the Shard development. The three projects, which included a new Northern line platform, have utilised the brick arch vaults beneath the station to incorporate extensive retail premises.

Bermondsey station is located on a corner site and makes use of extensive glazing to bring natural light into the building and percolate it down to platform level.

Jubilee line

The Jubilee line extension

—what it means for Jubilee line travellers

London Underground plans to extend the Jubilee line into south east and east London. A Bill is currently in Parliament to seek approval for this, the biggest addition to the Underground for twenty years, and services could be running by early 1996. The scheme involves constructing a new line from Green Park to Westminster, and through inner south London to Docklands.

The extension would open up a whole new range of destinations which could be reached direct by Jubilee —Westminster, (for the District and Circle lines) Waterloo (site of the Channel Tunnel terminal), London Bridge, three stations in London's rapidly growing Docklands and Stratford. Reaching these places presently involves one or more changes of train. Journey times would be cut greatly — Swiss Cottage to Canary Wharf would take about 25 minutes: Kingsbury to London Bridge around half an hour and West Hampstead to Westminster a little over a quarter of an hour.

Services on the extended Jubilee line would be speedy and frequent. Trains would normally run from north of Baker Street to Green Park, Westminster, Waterloo and then eastward to Docklands and Stratford.

An example of the publicity used to explain the benefits of the project.

Canada Water has an impressive circular surface building, which sits adjacent to the new bus station. An interchange with the the East London line (now part of the London Overground network) was also provided here.

Canary Wharf is probably the most spectacular station on the Jubilee Line Extension; the vast underground booking hall area alone being large enough to accommodate the Canary Wharf Tower. Sub-surface walkways connect the booking hall area with the adjacent office buildings and shopping malls, while a park sits between the station entrances above the station.

North Greenwich station sits alongside the O_2 arena, the former Millennium Dome, where a large public exhibition was held for the Millennium in 2000; the Jubilee line Extension was key to the success (or failure) of the enterprise. The distinctive station walkways here are clad in dark blue glass tiles, which provide a calming atmosphere. Three platforms enable trains from either Central London or Stratford to terminate here; the third platform was also built with an eye to facilitating a future extension towards the Royal Docks.

Canning Town is a surface station. Built on two levels, it incorporates connections with the DLR and the adjacent bus station. When it was originally constructed, two of the four DLR platforms were used by Silverlink services between Richmond and North Woolwich, before the Stratford to Canning Town section was transferred to the DLR.

West Ham is also a surface station and provides connections with the DLR (formerly Silverlink) as well as the District line, Hammersmith & City line and c2c rail services between Fenchurch Street and Shoeburyness via Southend.

Stratford is the final stop on the extension and also has three platforms. The station has seen a number of changes and continues to evolve as the surrounding area is redeveloped. The platform numbering system, however, has become confused due to the various alterations. Stratford now provides interchange with two DLR routes (one of which was previously part of the Silverlink route to North Woolwich), the Central line, Elizabeth line and London Overground as well as Greater Anglia and c2c rail services at weekends. There are also two bus stations and Stratford International station is a short walk away, which currently offers Southeastern High-Speed services between London St Pancras and Kent. The Queen Elizabeth Olympic Park and the Westfield Shopping Centre are nearby, as well as a number of other attractions plus a growing quantity of flats and office buildings. Stratford Market Depot, meanwhile, is located alongside the line between West Ham and Stratford.

Stratford Platform Numbers Today

Platform Number	Principal Operator	Comments
1	London Overground (Mildmay line)	New platform opened April 2009.
2	London Overground (Mildmay line)	New platform opened April 2009.
12	Greater Anglia	Also used by some London Overground services.
11	Greater Anglia	Also used by some London Overground services.
10A	Greater Anglia	Also incorporates Angel Lane freight loop.
10	Greater Anglia	
9	Greater Anglia	
8	Elizabeth line	Also used by some Greater Anglia services and c2c at weekends.
6	Central line	
5	Elizabeth line	Also used by some Greater Anglia services and c2c at weekends.
3	Central line	
3A	Central line	Additional platform funded by the Olympic Delivery Authority, opening in 2011.
4B	Docklands Light Railway	Canary Wharf branch.
4A	Docklands Light Railway	Canary Wharf branch.
13	Jubilee line	
14	Jubilee line	
15	Jubilee line	
16	Docklands Light Railway	Canning Town branch. Formerly the platform for North Woolwich services.
17	Docklands Light Railway	Canning Town branch. Formerly the platform for services from North Woolwich to Richmond.

Platforms are listed from north to south. Freight trains also pass through platforms 12, 11, 10A, 10, 9, 8, 6 and 5. Currently there is no platform 7.

The disused bay platforms alongside platforms 5 and 8 were originally constructed as part of the 1935–40 New Works Programme for a shuttle service between Stratford and Fenchurch Street. The bay platform alongside platform 5 was subsequently numbered platform 4 and was used by DLR services until these were transferred to platforms 4A and 4B.

Stratford International station has six platforms, two of which are used by the DLR and two by Southeastern. The remaining two platforms are designed for European services but were only used regularly during the 2012 Olympics and Paralympics.

A Jubilee line platform under construction at Waterloo station on 19 March 1997. (Derek Mulquin collection)

The Jubilee line crossover north of Waterloo station on 19 March 1997. (Derek Mulquin collection)

An escalator shaft under construction at Waterloo on 19 March 1997. (Derek Mulquin collection)

A Jubilee line tunnel under construction north of Waterloo on 19 March 1997. Note the narrow-gauge railway used for moving materials. (Derek Mulquin collection)

Schoma diesel locomotive No.8 at Canning Town during construction of the Jubilee Line Extension on 6 August 1996. (Malcolm Batten)

A Jubilee line train at Stratford during a test run on 3 April 1997. Services commenced between Stratford and North Greenwich on 14 May 1999. (Malcolm Batten)

A view of Stratford station on 8 June 2009. The Jubilee line platforms are on the left, while on the right, the former British Rail / Silverlink route to North Woolwich, closed in 2006, is in the process of being converted to DLR operation, including a northwards extension to Stratford International. Westfield shopping centre is under construction in the background. (Malcolm Batten)

Staged Opening

The Jubilee line was technically complicated, which led to some construction delays. Since the new line was a key component of plans to celebrate the year 2000 at the Millennium Dome at North Greenwich, it was essential that it opened on time.

It was decided that the New Austrian Tunnelling Method (NATM) would be used during construction, which involved sprayed concrete lining. The same tunnelling method was used for the Heathrow Express, which opened in 1998. On 21 October 1994, a tunnel collapse at Heathrow resulted in the NATM works on the Jubilee Line Extension being suspended between October 1994 and January 1995, while investigations were carried out.

The planned opening date of March 1998 was delayed by a variety of issues. A staged approach was taken, which enabled the new rolling stock and systems to be tested in a live environment ahead of the full opening.

The first section to open was between Stratford and North Greenwich on 14 May 1999. The line from North Greenwich to Bermondsey opened on 17 September and from Bermondsey to Waterloo on 24 September. The final part of the project was connecting the new railway with the existing line to Stanmore. On 19 November 1999, the short branch to Charing Cross was closed, with the full line opening between Stanmore and Stratford on the following day, 20 November.

The scheme had originally been budgeted at £1.9bn but the final cost was £3.2 billion, which included a private sector contribution.

Chapter 7

Depots and Sidings

Neasden Depot

Neasden Depot was opened by the Metropolitan Railway in 1882 and has been used for stabling Jubilee line rolling stock since 1979.

Significant work was undertaken at Neasden in 2010 and 2011 to prepare the depot for the new S stock trains being introduced on the Metropolitan line. The depot is still used for stabling Jubilee line trains, although all maintenance work is undertaken at Stratford Market.

The Jubilee line has typically stabled between 14 and 18 trains at Neasden.

Above: A train of 1972 Mark II stock passing Neasden Depot on 14 December 1986. (Malcolm Batten)

Opposite above: A train of 1996 stock passing Neasden Depot on 30 May 2016.

Opposite below: A train of 1996 stock passing Neasden Depot on 30 December 2023.

A mixture of Jubilee line 1972 stock and Metropolitan Line A stock at Neasden Depot on 16 June 1981. (Copyright TfL from the London Transport Museum Collection / Peter Wilson)

Stanmore Sidings

To facilitate the transfer of the Stanmore branch from the Bakerloo line to the Jubilee line, a new Bakerloo line depot was constructed at Stonebridge Park, and the existing seven stabling sidings at Stanmore were rebuilt to a ten-siding configuration. The project funding included new trains for the Fleet line.

1996 stock units stabled in the sidings at Stanmore on 26 July 2018.

Stanmore sidings and station on 16 June 2023.

A view of Stanmore sidings on 16 June 2023.

Stratford Market Depot

Several locations were investigated for a new depot to support the Jubilee Line Extension, including Thornton Fields, near Stratford, before the Stratford Market site was selected.

The £25m Stratford Market Depot opened in March 1998, following a five-year construction period. Designed by Wilkinson Eyre Architects (previously Chris Wilkinson Architects), the main depot building has a 100m (328ft) arched roof covering the eleven maintenance bays. There are also stabling sidings, office accommodation and a training centre.

Left: Two trains of 1996 stock stabled in the sidings at Stratford Market Depot on 7 July 2023.

Below: A train of 1996 stock stabled alongside the temporary three-road fit-out shed at Stratford Market on 7 July 2023.

Stratford Market Depot, seen from Abbey Road DLR station on 26 April 2004. At this stage, the 1996 stock consisted of six carriages. (Malcolm Batten)

The interior of Stratford Market Depot, which opened in March 1998. (Malcolm Batten collection)

Additional Stabling

The disused platforms at Charing Cross can also be used for stabling, although this is not planned on a regular basis.

Surrey Docks Depot

Located close to the current London Overground Silwood sidings, the depot would have provided additional capacity for Fleet line Stages 2, 3 and 4. The indicative drawings for the depot provided an eight-road stabling shed and a four-road maintenance shed, along with an outside washing road. Two reception sidings would have connected the depot with the Fleet line at Surrey Docks.

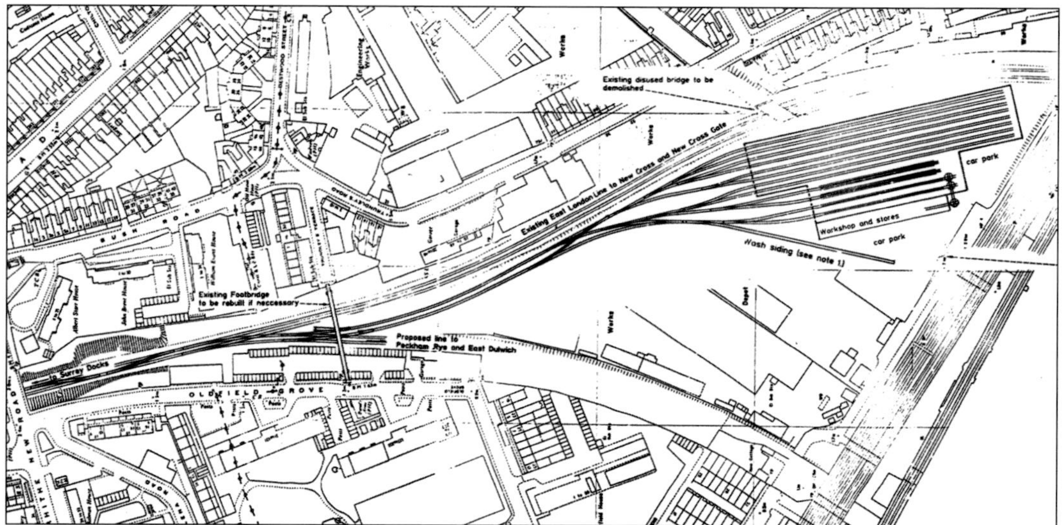

This plan shows the proposed layout of Surrey Docks Depot. Surrey Docks station (now Surrey Quays) is to the left-hand side of the drawing. The disused trackbed curving across the bottom of the drawing is shown as 'Proposed Line to Peckham Rye and East Dulwich'. (Copyright TfL from the TfL Engineering Records Collection)

Beckton Depot

The proposed depot at Beckton would have been located close to the site of the current DLR station at Beckton. It would have had around 25 roads, along with two engineers' sidings, and would have been an alternative to the other proposed depot at Custom House.

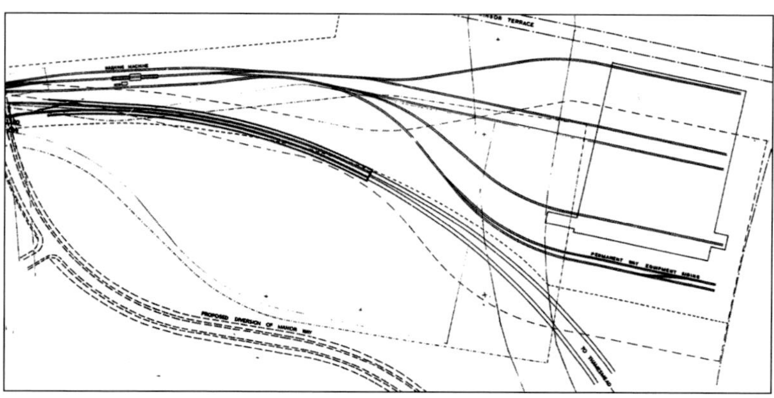

This plan shows the proposed layout of Beckton Depot. The road at the top right of the drawing is Winsor Way, while the road that curves from Beckton station to the bottom of the plan is shown as 'Proposed Diversion of Manor Way'. (Copyright TfL from the TfL Engineering Records Collection)

Custom House Depot

The main depot for the River line was initially going to be located at Custom House. Custom House station would have been provided with two island platforms and three tracks, enabling trains to terminate at, or start from, the station.

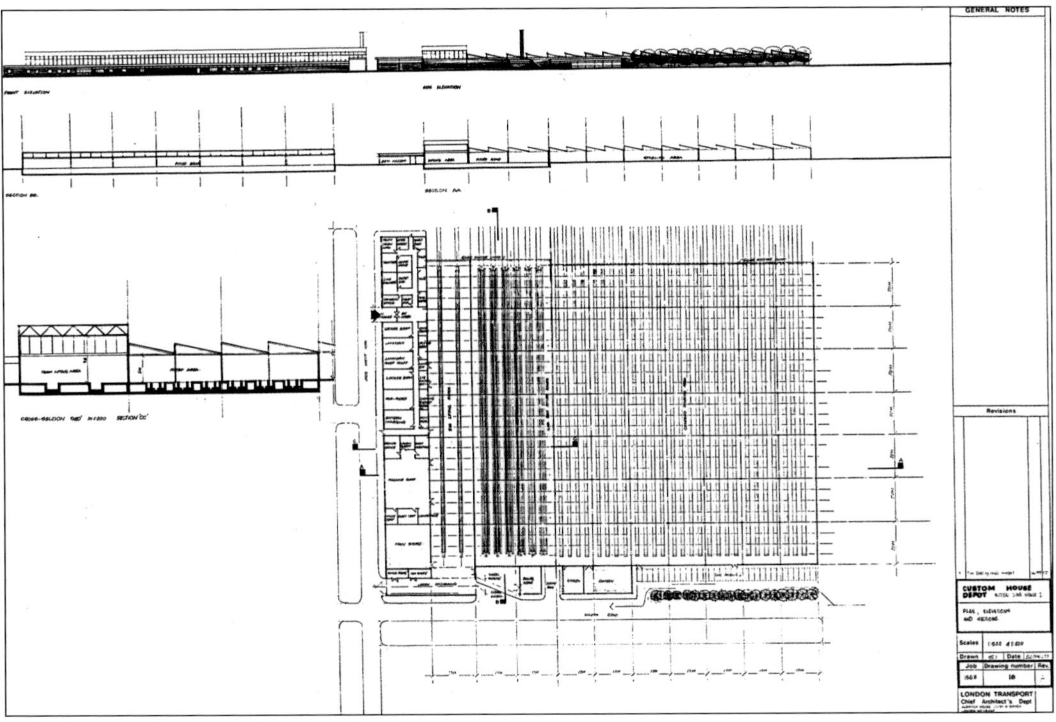

This plan shows the proposed depot building at Custom House. (Copyright TfL from the TfL Engineering Records Collection)

This plan shows the approaches to Custom House Depot. Custom House station is to the left of the drawing, with the main running lines passing above the depot. A carriage washer would have been provided, with the depot operations managed from a control tower. (Copyright TfL from the TfL Engineering Records Collection)

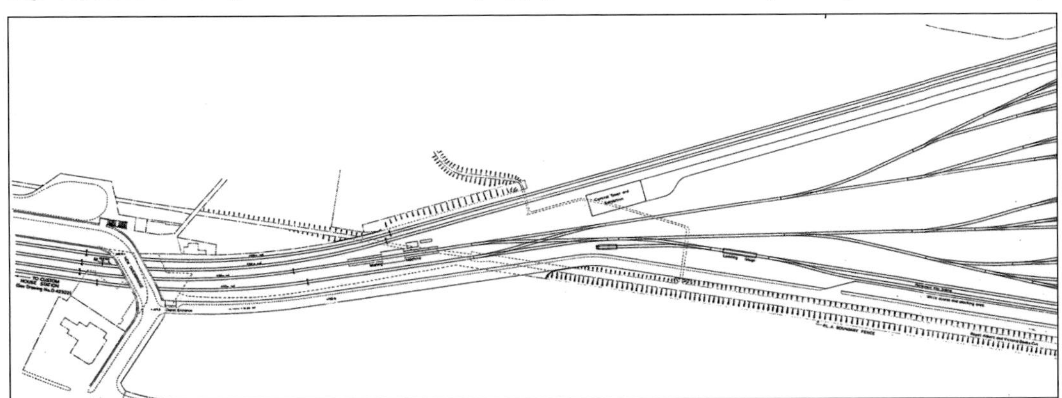

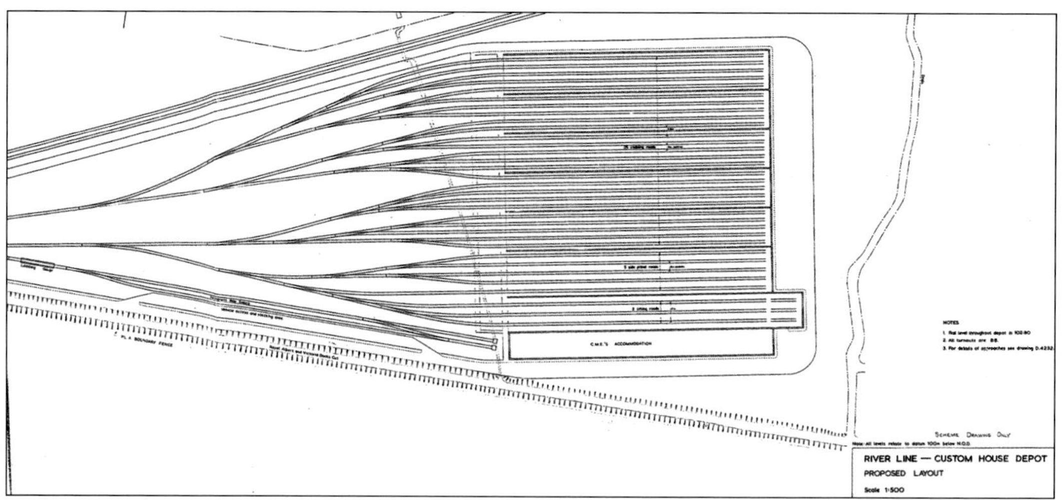

This plan shows the depot at Custom House, which would have had 25-five stabling roads, five pit roads and three lifting roads. Two engineering sidings would have been provided outside. (Copyright TfL from the TfL Engineering Records Collection)

Other Stabling Locations

Various additional stabling locations were considered, including Addiscombe (12 trains), Hayes (nine trains) and Kidbrooke (eight trains), which would have supported Stages 2 to 4 of the Fleet line.

Rolling Stock

1972 Stock (in service 1979–84)

In 1972, an order was placed for 32 new trains, known as 1972 Mark II stock. These units were very similar to the 1972 Mark I stock but had red-painted doors and some other minor differences.

The trains were used on the Bakerloo line, in advance of the Stanmore branch's transfer to the Jubilee line.

A 1972 Mk II stock unit, with carriage No 3543 leading, is at Kingsbury on 26 April 1979, working a Bakerloo line service to Elephant & Castle. From 1 May, this station became part of the Jubilee line and the destination of the train would have changed to Charing Cross. (Malcolm Batten)

1978 Stock

The initial plan was to order a fleet of more than 60 new trains for the Fleet line, which would have been sufficient for Stages 1 to 4 of the project. The 1978 stock was also referred to as the 'Tube Super Train'. Due to the uncertainty about the future stages of what became the Jubilee line, however, the order was not progressed.

1983 Stock (in service 1984–98)

In May 1982, an order was placed for 16 trains of 1983 stock. Built to a budget, they were fitted with single-leaf doors and began entering service in May 1984. A further 15 units (known as 1983 Mark II stock) were ordered in 1986, to supplement the initial fleet.

When the Jubilee Line Extension to Stratford was authorised, it was decided to procure a fleet of new trains, which would replace the 1983 stock wholesale.

The 1983 stock was to enjoy a very short life, the last train operating on the Jubilee line on 9 July 1998.

Above: A 1983-stock unit, with carriage No 3758 leading, calls at Kingsbury on 18 August 1996 with a service for Charing Cross. (Malcolm Batten)

Opposite above: A train of 1983 stock departing from Finchley Road in late 1985.

Opposite below: A train of 1983 stock on test at Northfields in autumn 1987.

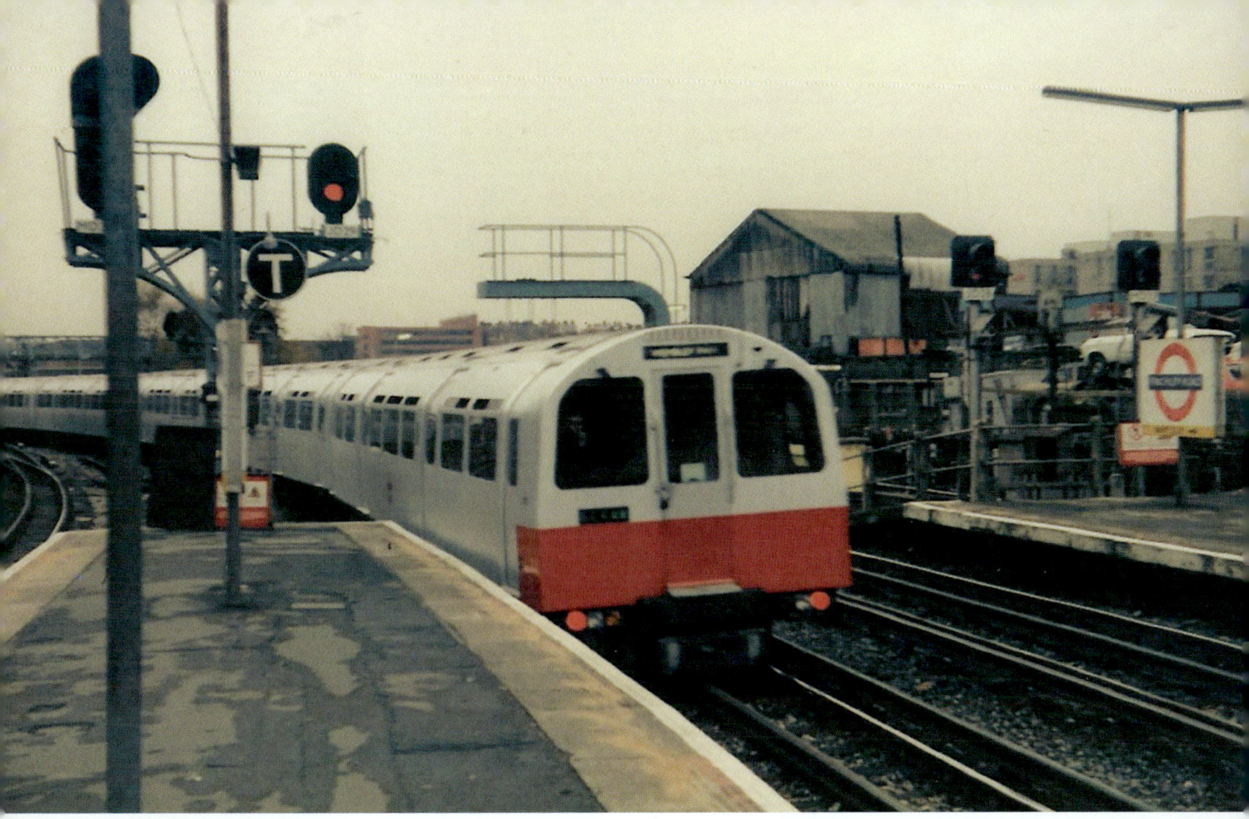

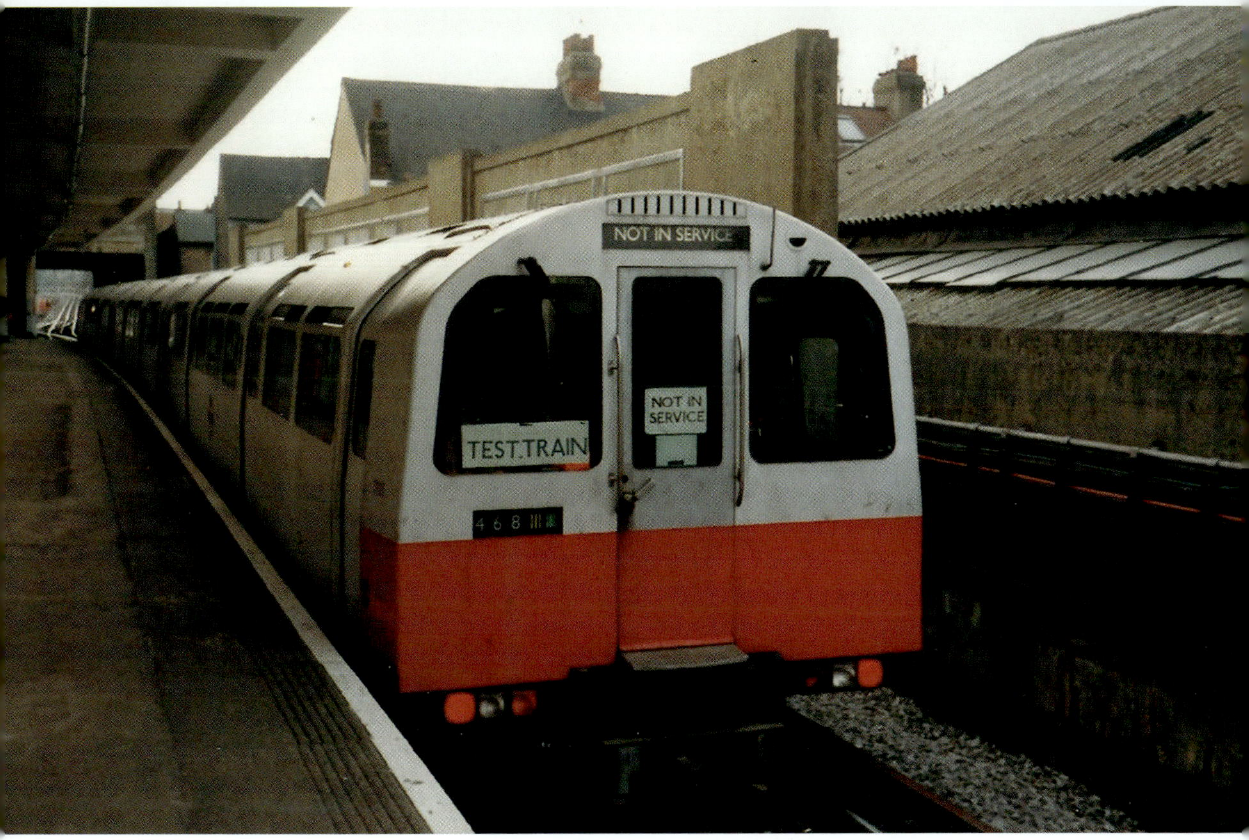

NOT IN SERVICE
NOT IN
SERVICE
TEST TRAIN

1996 Stock

The initial order was for 59 six-car trains, similar to the 1995 stock in service on the Northern line. The new trains were gradually introduced over 1997 and 1998, which was when the last of the 1983 stock was withdrawn.

Jubilee Line Seventh Car Project

The 1996 stock was originally constructed with six carriages. To increase capacity, an additional trailer carriage was ordered for each train, and these were inserted into the existing trains between December 2005 and January 2006. A number of modifications had to be carried out to the infrastructure, mainly at stations, to accommodate the longer trains.

In addition, four new trains were ordered, bringing the fleet size to 63 seven-carriage trains.

Left: On 26 July 1998, the train on the left is waiting in Wembley Park turnback siding, while a Southbound Jubilee line service passes on the right.

Below: A Jubilee line train passing the headshunt for Stratford Market Depot on 7 July 2023.

A train of 1996 stock approaching Kingsbury on 16 June 2023. The bridge in the background is a reminder that the Stanmore branch was originally constructed for Metropolitan line services, which had a larger loading gauge.

When London was bidding to host the 2012 Olympic and Paralympic Games, one of the Jubilee line trains was given 'Back the Bid' branding, and is seen at Stratford on 6 December 2004. Stratford station was also branded in this manner, as were a Class 315 train on the Liverpool Street to Shenfield line (now part of the Elizabeth line), a Docklands Light Railway train and 40 London buses. (Malcolm Batten)

Chapter 9

Stations

The stations along the Jubilee line date from four different time periods, showcasing the evolution of station design.

Stanmore

Stanmore was opened by the Metropolitan Railway on 10 December 1932 and consisted of an island platform, with stairs leading up to a street-level station building. This would have enabled a northern extension at a future date. The station transferred to the Bakerloo line on 20 November 1939 and then to the Jubilee line on 1 May 1979, along with the other stations on the Stanmore branch. A third platform was constructed to provide additional capacity following a resignalling project and opened in 2011.

Above: A train of 1996 stock standing in platform 2 at Stanmore on 26 July 2018. To the left is the original island platform, and to the right is the third platform, which opened in 2011.

Opposite above: Another view of Stanmore station, taken on 16 June 2023 and showing the original island platform to the left and the newer platform to the right.

Opposite below: The street-level station building at Stanmore was designed by Charles W. Clark and opened in 1932; it is seen on 16 June 2023. Stanmore once had a second station, located at the end of a branch line from Harrow & Wealdstone, but it closed to passengers in 1952 and to freight in 1964.

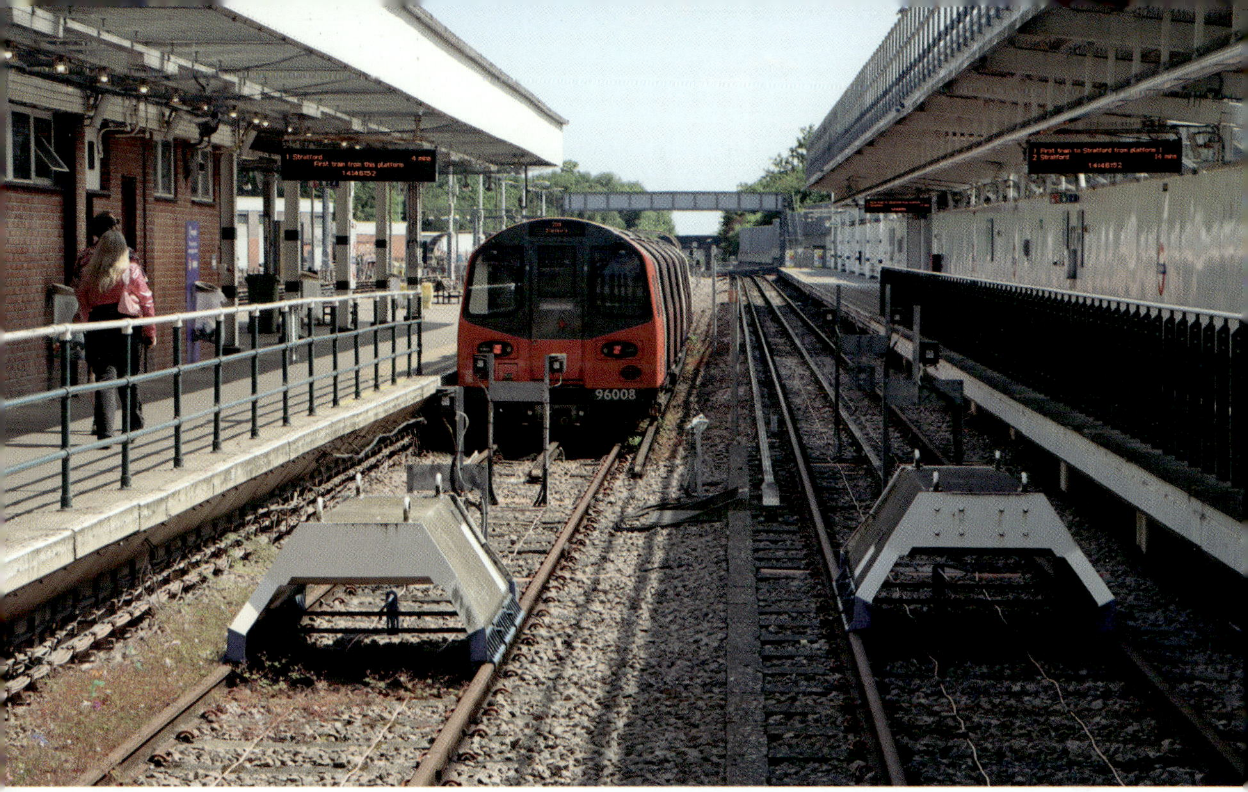

STANMORE STATION

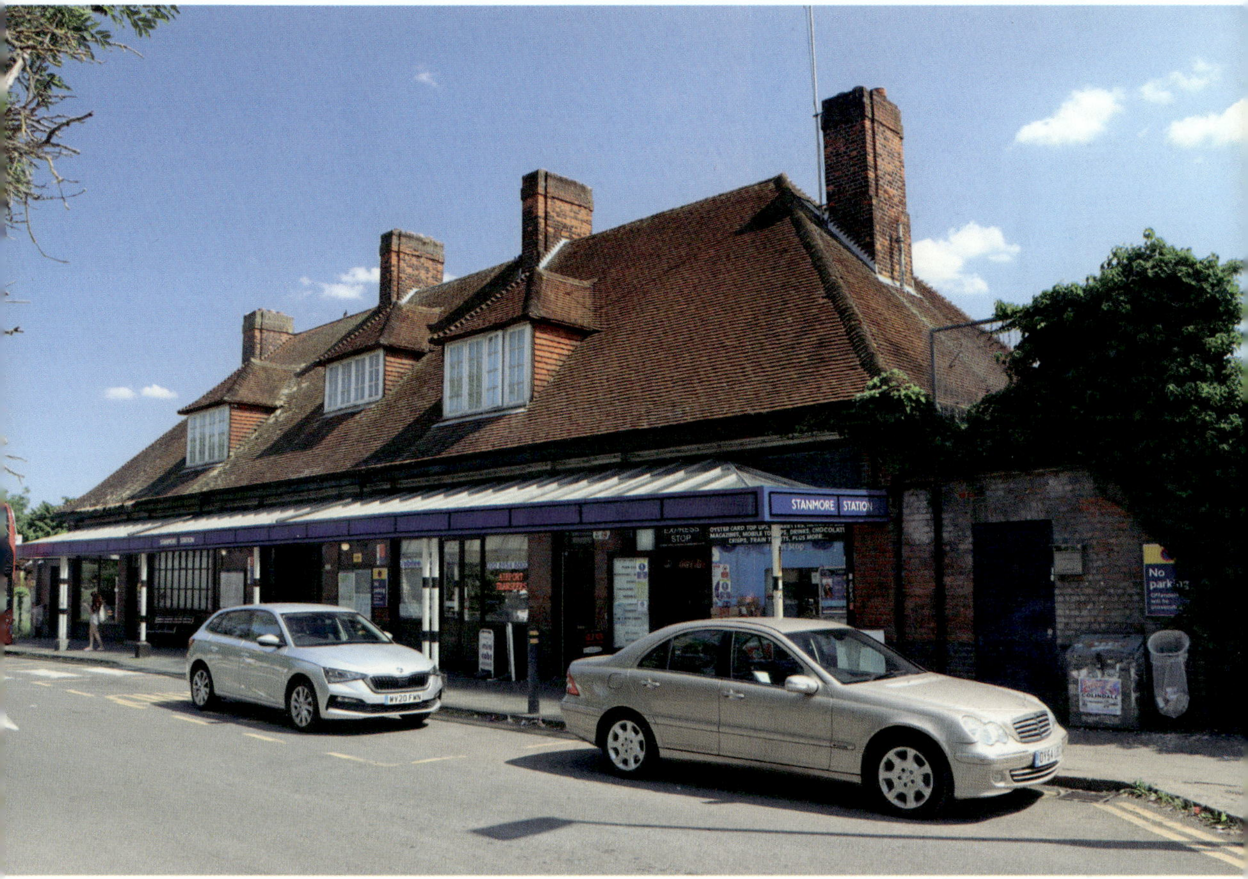

Canons Park

Canons Park was opened by the Metropolitan Railway as Canons Park (Edgware) on 10 December 1932. The two platforms are located on an embankment, with the station building at street level.

The Northbound platform at Canons Park, seen on 16 June 2023.

One of the two street-level entrances to Canons Park, seen on 16 June 2023.

Queensbury

Queensbury opened on 16 December 1934, a couple of years after the other stations on the Metropolitan Railway branch to Stanmore. The station sits on an embankment, with the station entrance at street level. A local estate agent selected the name to complement the nearby station at Kingsbury.

A train of 1996 stock departing from Queensbury on 16 June 2023, with a service for Stratford.

Kingsbury

Kingsbury station was opened on 10 December 1932 by the Metropolitan Railway. The platforms are in a cutting, with the surface building, designed by Charles W. Clark, located in a parade of shops. The station name dates from Saxon times.

Kingsbury station entrance, seen on 16 June 2023.

Trains of 1996 stock pass at Kingsbury on 16 June 2023.

Wembley Park

Wembley Park was opened by the Metropolitan Railway in 1893. The station has been extended several times over the years and now has six platforms, two of which are used by Jubilee line services. In 1924, Wembley hosted the British Empire Exhibition, which involved the construction of Wembley Stadium, and in 1934 the Empire Pool was built for the British Empire Games, later being converted to a concert venue known as Wembley Arena. Wembley Stadium and the Empire Pool were later used as venues during the 1948 London Olympics, which required some improvements to the station.

In 2007, Wembley stadium was rebuilt, including significant work to expand the station and provide a permanent event day entrance. The surrounding area has seen considerable development in recent years, including hotels, shops and residential buildings.

Trains of 1996 stock pass at Wembley Park on 16 June 2023.

A train of 1996 stock arriving at Wembley Park on 26 July 2018.

Neasden

Neasden station was opened by the Metropolitan Railway on 2 August 1880. The station was served by the Bakerloo line from 20 November 1939, with regular Metropolitan line services ceasing the following year. On 1 May 1979, it was transferred to the Jubilee line. There are four platforms, with the central island platform usually used by Jubilee line services. Neasden Depot is located between Wembley Park and Neasden.

A train of 1996 stock departing from Neasden for central London on 16 June 2023. The platform on the left sits alongside the Southbound Metropolitan line track and is not used on a regular basis.

A train of 1996 arriving at Neasden with a Stanmore service on 16 June 2023. The Metropolitan line Northbound track is on the right alongside the rarely used platform.

The road-level entrance to Neasden station, seen on 30 December 2023.

A train of 1996 stock departing from Neasden on 30 December 2023. The Jubilee line tracks are in the centre, either side of the island platform. The outer tracks are used by Metropolitan line services.

Dollis Hill

Dollis Hill was opened on 1 October 1909 by the Metropolitan Railway and had an island platform. The station was rebuilt to designs by Stanley Heaps as part of the 1935–1940 New Works Programme, in advance of the transfer of services to the Bakerloo line in 1939. There is one island platform. Metropolitan line and Chiltern Railways services pass the station but do not call.

Dollis Hill station was rebuilt in 1938 and is seen on 16 June 2023.

A Northbound train of 1996 stock arriving at Dollis Hill on 16 June 2023. The Northbound Metropolitan line track is to the right, with the pair of tracks used by the Chiltern line beyond.

The platform-level building at Dollis Hill was rebuilt in 1938, prior to the commencement of Bakerloo line services. Metropolitan line services ceased to call in 1940. The Metropolitan line tracks are situated either side of the Jubilee line tracks, seen on 26 July 2018.

Willesden Green

Willesden Green was opened on 24 November 1879, although the current street-level building dates from 1925. As with many of the other Metropolitan Railway stations of the same period, it was designed by Charles W. Clark. The station was served by the Bakerloo line from 20 November 1939, with regular Metropolitan line services ceasing the following year. Jubilee line services now call at the central island platform, which is flanked by the Metropolitan line tracks. The platforms alongside the Metropolitan line tracks are not used on a regular basis.

A Northbound train arriving at Willesden Green on 16 June 2023. The right-hand platform, which sits alongside the Metropolitan line track, is now home to some impressive floral displays.

The impressive surface-level station building at Willesden Green, complete with Metropolitan Railway signage, is seen on 16 June 2023.

Kilburn

Kilburn opened as Kilburn & Brondesbury on 24 November 1879. The station was rebuilt in 1916 and saw further changes before transferring to the Bakerloo line in 1939, with Metropolitan line services ceasing the following year. The station originally had two side platforms, but the original Southbound platform was converted to an island platform, which is used by Jubilee line services today, and the former Northbound platform was demolished.

A Northbound Jubilee line service arriving at Kilburn on 16 June 2023. The Metropolitan line Northbound platform was once located on the right-hand side, alongside the Northbound Metropolitan line track.

The street-level entrance to Kilburn station, which is sandwiched between two bridges, seen on 16 June 2023.

A Southbound Jubilee line train calling at West Hampstead on 13 March 2022. Although not physically connected, West Hampstead London Overground station and West Hampstead Thameslink station are both a short distance away.

West Hampstead

West Hampstead opened on 30 June 1879 and originally had two side platforms. The Southbound platform was converted into an island platform in 1897, to provide space for widening the formation. The station was rebuilt in 1938 ahead of its transfer to the Bakerloo line in 1939, with Metropolitan line services ceasing to call in 1940.

Finchley Road

Finchley Road was opened by the Metropolitan Railway on 30 June 1879. The station originally had two platforms, but was rebuilt with four platforms in 1914, with further changes made in 1939 ahead of Bakerloo line services commencing. The station has two island platforms, one for Northbound Jubilee and Metropolitan line services and one for Southbound trains. The station provides a useful cross-platform interchange between Metropolitan and Jubilee line services.

A Northbound Jubilee line train of 1996 stock arriving at Finchley Road on 16 June 2023. The Jubilee line uses the central two tracks, with the outer platforms served by Metropolitan line trains.

A Southbound Jubilee line train departing from Finchley Road on 26 July 2018.

Swiss Cottage

The new tunnels were built as part of the 1935–1940 New Works Programme, with the Bakerloo line trains taking over the stopping services between Baker Street and Stanmore from 1939. The three intermediate Metropolitan line stations were replaced by two new Bakerloo line stations at Swiss Cottage and St John's Wood, both of which had a very distinctive style. Swiss Cottage opened on 20 November 1939 and was served by Bakerloo line services until the route transferred to the Jubilee line on 1 May 1979.

The stylish 1930s-style uplighters remain in use on the escalators at Swiss Cottage, seen on 30 December 2023. With the rapid expansion of Metroland, the Metropolitan line was left with a severe bottleneck between Finchley Road and Baker Street, where four tracks narrowed to two. This was exacerbated by the three intermediate stations at Swiss Cottage, Marlborough Road and Lord's (previously called St John's Wood). The solution was to build duplicate tube tunnels and close the intermediate stations, although the original intention was to retain Lord's for special events.

The atmospheric escalators and signage remain at Swiss Cottage, seen here on 30 December 2023.

As seen on 30 December 2023, Swiss Cottage retains the original tiling at platform level.

A train of 1996 stock arriving at Swiss Cottage on 30 December 2023.

St John's Wood

St John's Wood opened on 20 November 1939, replacing the nearby Metropolitan line station at Lord's, which was closed. Designed by Stanley Heaps, the station was originally called Acacia Road, or Acacia, but was changed to St John's Wood before opening. A residential building was built above the station in the early 1960s. As with Swiss Cottage, St John's Wood has two platforms and has been served by the Jubilee line since 1 May 1979.

Seen on 1 July 2017, the distinctive station building at St John's Wood, which opened on 20 November 1939.

A number of heritage features remain at St John's Wood, as seen on 1 July 2017.

Baker Street

Baker Street station opened on 10 January 1863 as part of the world's first underground railway between Farringdon Street and Paddington. The station has seen many changes over the years and now has ten platforms. The Bakerloo line opened on 10 March 1906 and Stanmore services commenced on 20 November 1939, utilising the new tunnels between Baker Street and Finchley Road. An additional Southbound platform was constructed at the same time, to enable Stanmore and Watford Junction services to be regulated. A fourth platform was constructed for Northbound Jubilee line services prior to opening on 1 May 1979. The platform and subway tiling incorporates a silhouette of the fictional detective Sherlock Holmes.

Seen on 16 June 2023, Baker Street station's entrance facing Marylebone Road, including Chiltern Court, which was constructed above the station in 1929.

A Southbound Jubilee line train at Baker Street on 16 June 2023. A short passageway connects with the parallel Southbound Bakerloo line platform.

Bond Street

Bond Street station was opened on 24 September 1900 by the Central London Railway (now the Central line). Further changes were made in the 1920s, followed five decades later by renewed expansion to incorporate the Jubilee line. This involved the construction of a large ramp over the roadway to enable the construction of the expanded station while ensuring minimal impact on road traffic above. More changes came along ahead of the Elizabeth line's opening. Though passenger services commenced on 24 May 2022, the Elizabeth line platforms didn't open until 24 October. The Jubilee line platforms retain their original panelling and tiles depicting a carefully wrapped parcel, reflecting the nearby shopping district.

As a Stratford service departs Bond Street on 16 June 2023, the original 1970s panelling is still evident.

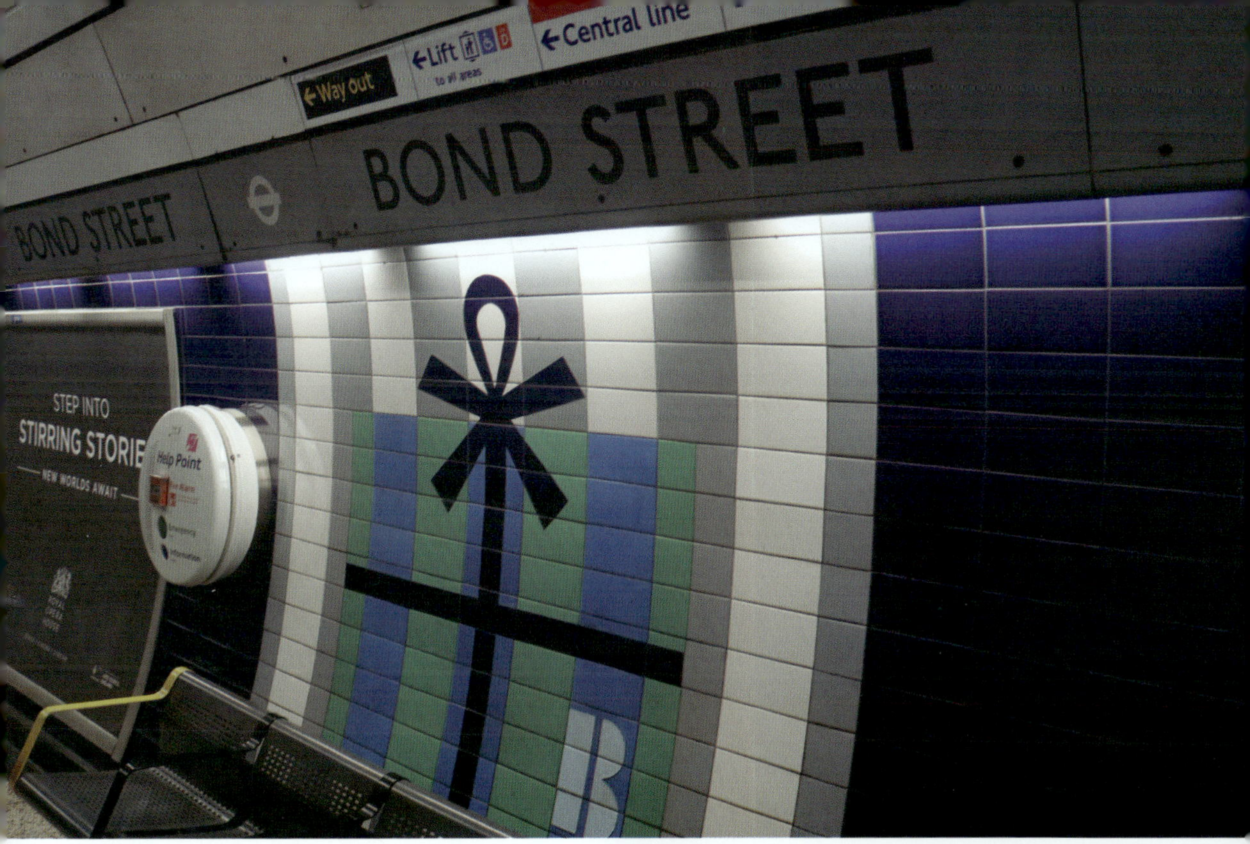

Above: The distinctive platform tiling at Bond Street on 16 June 2023.

Right: Bond Street was temporarily renamed Burberry Street for London Fashion Week, as seen on 19 September 2023.

In contrast with the rather austere Victoria line platforms of the 1960s, the Jubilee line platforms at Green Park are colourful, as seen here on 16 June 2023.

Green Park

Green Park was opened on 15 December 1906 as Dover Street. The station was renamed Green Park on 18 September 1933 and was served by the Piccadilly line alone until 7 March 1969, when the Victoria line platforms opened. The Jubilee line joined the group on 1 May 1979.

Westminster

Westminster station opened on 24 December 1868 and was served by the District and Circle lines until 22 December 1999, when the Jubilee line opened.

The original plans for Westminster station were modified after concerns were raised about the disruption that would have been caused during construction. It was still a complicated process, with ground movements carefully monitored to avoid any damage to the Elizabeth Tower.

The station is on a compact site, with the eastbound platform located above the westbound platform. The Circle and District line platforms were reconstructed at the same time. This view was taken on 23 June 2023.

Waterloo

The main line station at Waterloo has 24 platforms, with the adjacent station at Waterloo East having a further four (numbered A to D). Below ground, there are eight further platforms serving the Bakerloo line, Jubilee line, Northern line and Waterloo & City line. Plans to extend the Piccadilly line to Waterloo were not progressed. The first line to open here was the Waterloo & City line, although this was built and operated by the London & South Western Railway, eventually transferring to London Underground on 5 April 1994. Connecting the Jubilee line to Waterloo and Waterloo East was very complicated, especially as the main line station needed to stay operational, but when this was accomplished, services began on 24 September 1999.

Right: Seen on 23 June 2023, Waterloo's new Jubilee line entrance on Waterloo Road utilised part of the colonnade, which was previously used as a bus stand. The roof gives away the new and the old areas of the ticket hall.

Below: A balcony connects the Jubilee line ticket hall with the Waterloo & City line, facilitating this 30 June 2023 view of the Waterloo Road entrance.

Southwark

Southwark opened on 20 November 1999, a few months after Waterloo's Jubilee line station. The station entrance is on Blackfriars Road, but it is also connected to the four platforms at Waterloo East.

Southwark station is only a short distance from Waterloo, but provides a useful connection with Waterloo East station. The eastbound platform is quiet on 23 June 2023, enabling a clear view of the platform screen doors (PSDs) that were first used in London on the Jubilee Line Extension.

Southwark station entrance has a unique design and was built to enable future development of the area above the building. Beneath the railway bridge on the right, you can see the entrance to Blackfriars station, which was opened by the South Eastern Railway (SER) in 1864. It closed in 1869 when the current Waterloo East station opened. This view was taken on 23 June 2023.

Natural light was used where possible, illuminating the escalators that lead down to the Jubilee line platforms. This view is from 23 June 2023.

The new station at Southwark wraps itself around the original viaduct and provides a useful connection with Waterloo East station, as seen on 23 June 2023.

Left: The stations on the Jubilee Line Extension were very different to previous Underground stations and won many awards; this view of Southwark is of 23 June 2023.

Below: The entrance to the Jubilee line station at Southwark, located at the east end of platform D at Waterloo East. This picture was taken on 23 June 2023.

The platforms at Waterloo main line station are numbered 1 to 24, while the four platforms at Waterloo East are designated A to D. Seen on 23 June 2023, the new canopy on platforms B and C covers the staircase leading to Southwark station, contrasting with the older canopy behind.

London Bridge

London Bridge underground station opened on 25 February 1900, when the City and South London Railway extended to Moorgate. This precipitated the closure of King William Street station. The Jubilee line arrived here on 7 October 1999, but the station has carried on growing, with changes both above ground and below. Its status as an important interchange has increased since the opening of Thameslink and construction of the Shard skyscraper.

Seen on 30 December 2023, the underground platforms on the Jubilee Line Extension have a very distinctive style, including the perch seats seen on the left and the platform screen doors seen on the right.

The wide circulation area at London Bridge sits between the Jubilee line platforms in this view of 30 December 2023. The stairs lead to the Northern line, with escalators visible at the far end of the concourse.

The entrance to London Bridge Underground station on Tooley Street, located beneath the arches of the main line station, as seen on 30 December 2023.

The tunnel linings were completed with metal plates, incorporating the London Bridge station name; these are seen alongside a traditional roundel sign on 30 December 2023.

Bermondsey

Bermondsey is in an area previously poorly served by rail services. The modest station building hides the station below, with natural light just reaching the platforms.

The platform screen doors (PSDs) can be seen clearly in this view of 23 June 2023, creating a barrier between the train and the platform. The PSDs on the Jubilee line do not extend right up to the ceiling, unlike those installed more recently on the Elizabeth line.

Natural light just about reaches the platforms at Bermondsey station, seen here on 23 June 2023.

The austere entrance to Bermondsey station, seen on 23 June 2023. The station was designed to permit an office building to be constructed above it at a future date.

The interior of the station, seen here on 23 June 2023, is more pleasant, with natural light filling the entrance and concourse area.

Canada Water

Canada Water opened on 17 September 1999 and included new platforms on the East London line, now the Windrush line, which forms part of the London Overground network.

Canada Water station provides an interchange with the Windrush line, which is part of the wider London Overground network. Construction of the station was very challenging, involving cutting into the original brick-lined East London line tunnels in order to provide two new platforms on the East London line (then part of the London Underground) as well as the two Jubilee line platforms. The East London line platforms were built at right angles to the Jubilee line platforms below. The East London line platforms opened on 19 August 1999, with the Jubilee line platforms following suit on 17 September. This picture was taken on 23 June 2023.

The wide platform-level concourse that sits between the Jubilee line platforms, seen here on 23 June 2023.

The station building constructed at Canada Water initially provided an interchange with the East London line. This closed on 22 December 2007 to enable the line to be upgraded and incorporated into the London Overground network. The London Overground platforms reopened on 27 April 2010, with the full service commencing on 23 May. Transport for London still manages this section of the London Overground network, with the remainder controlled by Network Rail. This picture was taken on 23 June 2023.

The distinctive drum-shaped building at Canada Water on 23 June 2023, with the bus station sitting alongside. This part of London Overground was renamed the Windrush line in 2024.

Canary Wharf

The Docklands Light Railway had been constructed to meet initial transport needs in the heart of the new financial district that boomed following deregulation of the financial markets in 1986, but it soon became apparent that a full-size underground railway was needed, hence the Jubilee Line Extension of a decade later. Canary Wharf station, within its own box a short distance from the DLR station, opened on 17 September 1999. The Elizabeth line station, a short distance away from both previous stations of this name, followed in 2022.

After the Jubilee line (River line) extension to Thamesmead was dropped in the early 1980s, plans were drawn up for a lower-cost alternative. This resulted in the construction of the Docklands Light Railway that opened in 1987, although the DLR station at Canary Wharf opened later. The DLR has been upgraded several times, but it became clear that the area needed a full-size underground railway. This view is of the Jubilee line platform-level concourse, taken on 19 September 2023.

One of the Jubilee line station entrances at Canary Wharf, seen on 19 September 2023.

Below the surface at Canary Wharf, a vast concourse area is provided, including access to the adjacent offices and shopping centre. A park sits above the station, providing some green space amid the tower blocks, as in this view of 19 September 2023.

The second main entrance to Canary Wharf station, with the park behind, and the 2013 stamp marking the 150th anniversary of the London Underground.

Above: The second main entrance to Canary Wharf station seen on 19 September 2023, with the park behind.

Right: To mark the 150th anniversary of the London Underground, a set of stamps was issued in 2013, one of which featured the Jubilee line station at Canary Wharf.

North Greenwich

North Greenwich was designed with three platforms, which enable trains from both directions to reverse here. This is particularly useful when large events are taking place in the adjacent O₂ Arena. The third platform would also facilitate a future branch line into the Royal Docks, although there are no current plans for this.

North Greenwich station enjoys a distinctive design, with blue glazed tiles providing a calming experience for passengers, as seen here on 26 November 2023.

The station opened on 14 May 1999, in time for the following year's exhibition at the Millennium Dome. The Jubilee line Extension crosses three times beneath the River Thames on its way here, and will do so a fourth time to reach Stratford.

Canning Town

Canning Town has six platforms on two levels. Four of them are served by the DLR, with the remaining two having been used by Jubilee line trains since 14 May 1999.

When the current Canning Town station opened, it provided a connection between the Jubilee line, Docklands Light Railway and the National Rail service to North Woolwich, which was then operated by Silverlink. The National Rail line closed on 9 December 2006 before reopening on 31 August 2011 as part of the DLR extension to Stratford International. The station is built on two levels, with the DLR platforms sitting parallel to that line and above the Jubilee line. This view was taken on 23 August 2020.

West Ham

West Ham has eight platforms, serving the Jubilee line, DLR, District line, Hammersmith & City line and main line services operated by c2c. DLR and Jubilee line trains pass beneath the other lines at a right angle. The station opened on 1 May 1901, with underground services commencing on 2 June 1902; Jubilee line trains called from 14 May 1999.

This view of West Ham station on 8 August 2020 shows a 1996 stock train arriving at West Ham from Stratford. The Jubilee line platforms are finished in brick.

Stratford

Stratford is now the fifth busiest railway station in the United Kingdom, after Liverpool Street, Paddington, Tottenham Court Road and Waterloo. Major changes were made to the station to incorporate the Jubilee Line Extension, with further enhancements ahead of the London 2012 Olympic Games and concurrent construction of the Westfield shopping centre; changes most recently have been to accommodate the Elizabeth line.

Above: Stratford station has changed beyond recognition in the last three decades. This new concourse was constructed for the Jubilee Line Extension and is seen here on 7 July 2023. It is bisected by the DLR's line to Stratford International, while the three Jubilee line platforms are to the right.

Opposite above: In 1988, plans were drawn up to expand the main line station at Stratford to accommodate the Jubilee line. Two new platforms would have been constructed for Jubilee line services, parallel to the present-day platform 3A (westbound Central line). The platforms would have been located roughly where the staircases are in the above picture. A new station building would have been constructed on Station Street, in the 'V' between the North London line platforms (now used by DLR services) and the new Jubilee line platforms. The proposals would have included what is now platform 3A, providing a cross-platform interchange between the Central and Jubilee lines. The Jubilee line platforms would have been configured for through services, facilitating some of the options considered by the Central London Rail Study. The railway would have entered tunnels either side of Stratford, with a turnback siding located to the east of the station. Two new platforms would have been built for the DLR, near to the site of the present-day platforms 4A and 4B, although side platforms would have been provided rather than an island. (Copyright TfL from the TfL Engineering Records Collection)

Opposite below: A train of 1996 stock arriving at Stratford on 30 June 2018. The office behind is used by train crew and supports the 'stepping back' arrangements that minimise station reversal times.

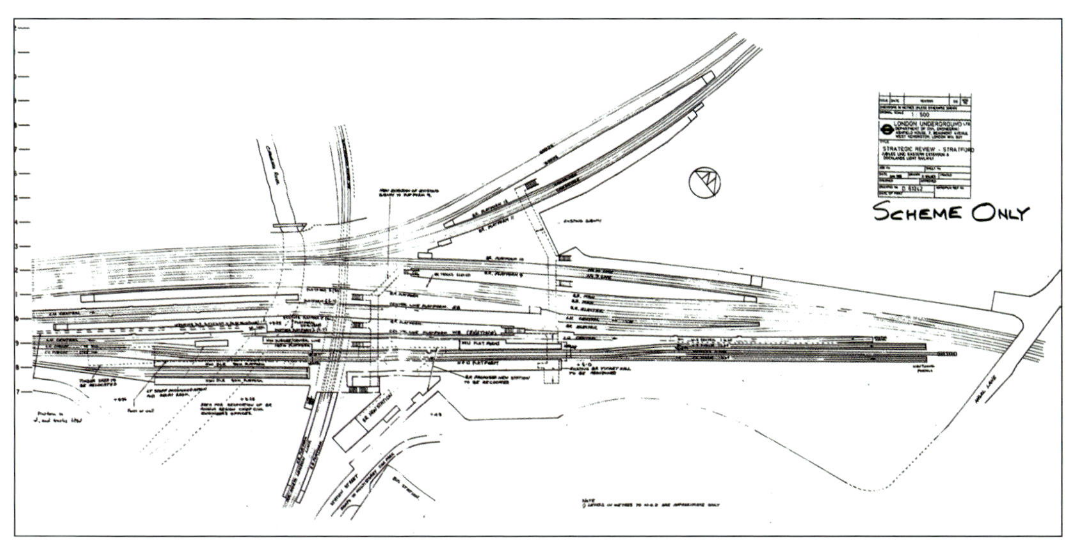

1 : 500
LONDON UNDERGROUND LTD
STRATEGIC REVIEW - STRATFORD
D 63242
SCHEME ONLY

Jubilee line
96105

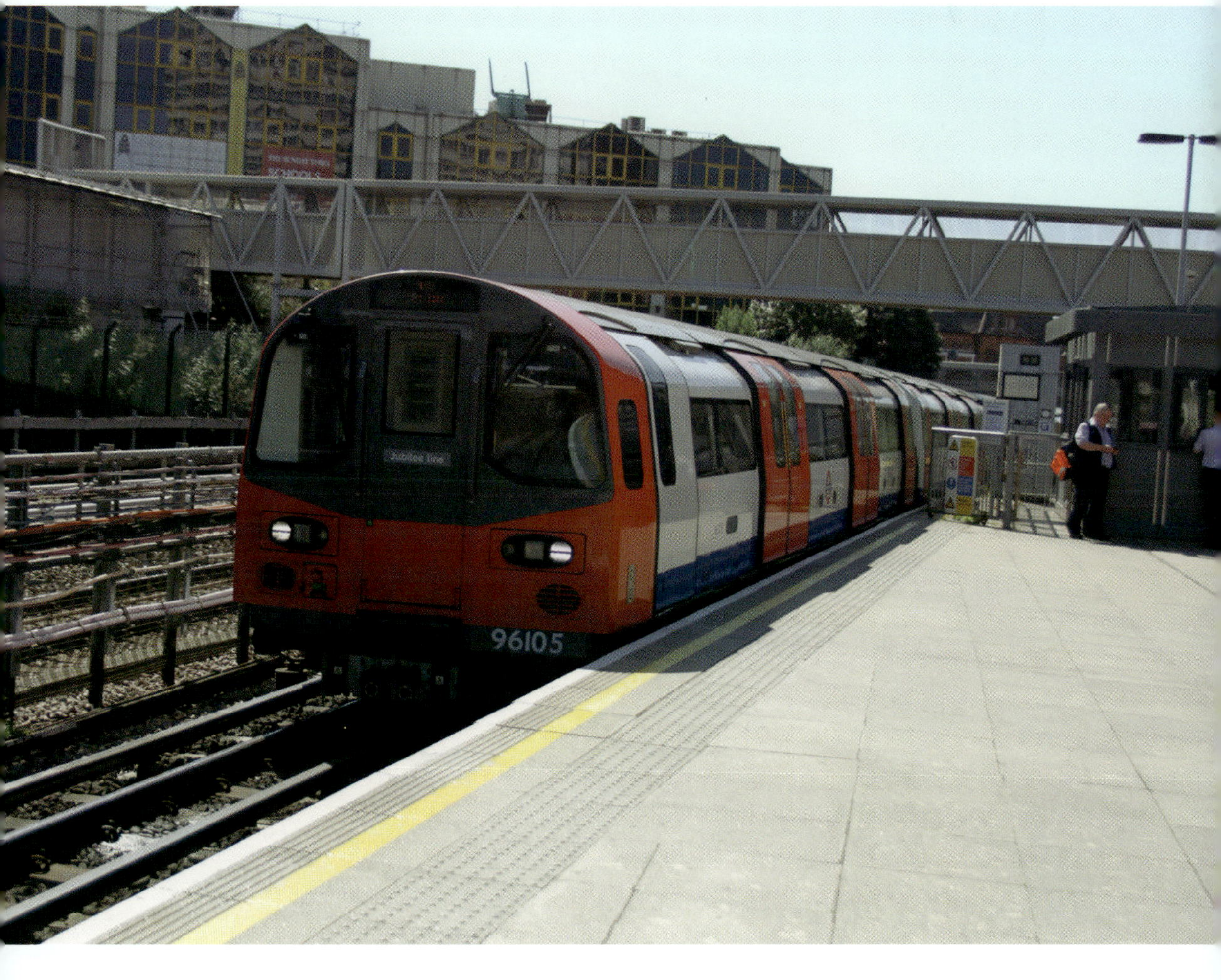

Two trains of 1996 stock at Stratford on 3 January 2016.

Chapter 10

Running the Railway

The Railway Signalling Centre was located at Baker Street and was shared with the Metropolitan line due to common infrastructure between Finchley Road and Wembley Park. A new centre was built at Neasden for the Jubilee Line Extension, with a plan to introduce automatic train operation (ATO) when the extension opened, but due to delays with introducing the new signalling technology, the JLE commenced with conventional signalling.

The railway between Stanmore and Green Park was controlled from the existing facility at Baker Street, with the Green Park to Stratford section controlled from Neasden. In 2011, the new Seltrac moving block signalling system was introduced along with full ATO. This enabled the whole railway to be controlled from Neasden, giving a service of up to 30 trains per hour in each direction.

In October 2016, the Jubilee line was added to the 'Night Tube', which provided a ten-minute interval overnight service between Stratford and Stanmore on Friday and Saturday nights.

The Jubilee line is 37.2km long (just over 23 miles) with 27 stations.

The underground stations on the Jubilee Line Extension are provided with platform screen doors, marking the first use of this technology in the United Kingdom. A similar system has been installed in the underground stations on the Elizabeth line. This is London Bridge on 1 September 2019.

The Jubilee line signalling control centre at Neasden, seen on 30 December 2023.

A train of 1996 stock departing from Neasden towards Wembley Park on 30 December 2023.

A train of 1996 stock negotiating the complex track layout at Neasden on 30 December 2023.

Reversing Facilities

The original plans for the Jubilee Line Extension would have seen a reversing siding east of London Bridge and a second east of Canary Wharf, along with a crossover at Waterloo for emergency use.

These proposals were later amended, partly due to construction and design challenges, and instead a trailing crossover was provided west of Waterloo and a facing crossover west of London Bridge. Scissors crossovers were provided west of Canary Wharf to enable trains to terminate there if required.

The biggest change was at North Greenwich, which was expanded to include a third platform, thus providing a turnback facility and additional capacity to support events at the Millennium Dome. The redesign of North Greenwich enabled the junction for a future branch to the Royal Docks to be incorporated within the station design, rather than a separate 'step-plate' junction that was originally proposed.

Stratford was originally designed with two platforms, but this was later amended to three. As part of the resignalling project, a third platform was also constructed at Stanmore at the other end of the line. The work was completed in 2009, but the platform was not used until 2011, when the new signalling system was commissioned.

It is still possible to reverse Jubilee line trains in the disused platforms at Charing Cross, although passengers need to alight at Green Park.

Turnback sidings are Wembley Park, Willesden Green and West Hampstead. Trains also regularly terminate or start from Canons Park, Neasden and West Ham before proceeding to and from the sidings.

Stepping Back

To maintain the service frequency, train drivers usually leave the train when it reaches its destination, and a new driver works the service back out. This avoids the need for a driver to 'change ends' and reduces the turnaround time at destinations.

A view just south of Willesden Green station where the Jubilee line tracks are flanked by the Metropolitan line and Chiltern line. (Malcolm Batten)

A train of 1996 stock standing in the reversing siding at Wembley Park on 16 June 2023.

A train of 1996 stock preparing to leave the reversing siding at Wembley Park on 26 July 2018.

A train of 1996 stock departing from the reversing siding at Willesden Green on 16 June 2023.

Chapter 11
Recent Developments

The Elizabeth line opened on 24 May 2022, providing interchanges with the Jubilee line at Bond Street and Stratford. The new line also has a station at Canary Wharf, although it is not physically connected to the DLR or Jubilee line stations.

The station at Bond Street was expanded to accommodate the Elizabeth line and provide suitable connections to the Jubilee and Central line platforms.

Stratford station has become one of the busiest on the national rail network, being served by the Jubilee line, Central line, Elizabeth line, two DLR routes and the London Overground (Mildmay line) as well as National Rail services operated by c2c and Greater Anglia. Stratford International station is a short distance away, providing high-speed services operated by Southeastern between London and Kent. There are also two bus stations at Stratford, one at each side of the railway.

Plans exist in the short, medium and long term to improve and expand the station facilities at Stratford. On 10 July 2024 a new station entrance leading to Gibbons Road opened, providing easier access to the Jubilee line platforms.

Left: Stratford's new Gibbons Road entrance under construction on 7 July 2023.

Below: Gibbons Road entrance, seen the day after it opened on 11 July 2024.

Chapter 12

Future Plans

There are no current plans to replace the Jubilee line's 1996 stock, despite the trains approaching their 30th birthdays. Even so, a mid-life refurbishment has been completed, which will extend their life.

Now seemingly unlikely to progress are proposals for extending the DLR westward from Bank, utilising the disused Jubilee line tunnels at Charing Cross. The platforms there have been used in films, most notably the James Bond film *Skyfall* (2012) and television programmes, while regular 'Hidden London' tours to these platforms have been operated by The London Transport Museum.

In the middle of the line, North Greenwich station has passive provision for an extension towards the Royal Docks, but this is less likely to progress now that the Elizabeth line has opened. However, a DLR extension from Beckton to Thamesmead is a long-standing aspiration, more recently having had a further extension to Abbey Wood tacked on.

An original painting of the abandoned Jubilee line platforms at Charing Cross. (Karen Brown)

Opening and Closing Dates

Jubilee Line Opening Dates

Route / Station	Opened	Comments
Charing Cross–Stanmore	1 May 1979	Finchley Road–Stanmore originally opened by the Metropolitan Railway on 10 December 1932. Baker Street–Stanmore operated by Bakerloo line between 20 November 1939 and 30 April 1979. Baker Street–Charing Cross new construction.
Stratford–North Greenwich	14 May 1999	
Bermondsey–North Greenwich	17 September 1999	
Bermondsey–Waterloo	24 September 1999	
Waterloo–Green Park	20 November 1999	

Jubilee Line Closure Dates

Route / Station	Closed	Comments
Charing Cross–Green Park	19 November 1999	Retained for reversing empty trains and stabling.

* Short-term closures are not shown.

Further Reading

Books and Booklets

A to Z of London Underground Stations, Jason Cross, Train Crazy Publishing, 2019

Delivering the JLE, Antony Oliver and Adrian Greeman, New Civil Engineer, 1999

Developing London's Docklands – Another Great Planning Disaster, Sue Brownhill, Paul Chapman Publishing Limited, 1990

East London Railways: From Docklands to Crossrail, Malcolm Batten, Amberley Publishing, 2000

Extending the Jubilee Line, Jon Willis, London Transport, 1997

Jubilee Line Seventh Car Project, Tube Lines, 2005

Jubilee Line Extension, Mike Winney, Antony Oliver, Dave Parker, Helena Russell and Ty Byrd, New Civil Engineer, 1996

Jubilee Line Extension – from concept to completion, Bob Mitchell, Thomas Telford Publishing, 2003

Improvements to the Jubilee Line – Work at Stanmore Station, Tube Lines, 2004

London Rail – A Guide to TfL's Depots and Stabling Points, Paul Jordan and Paul Smith, Crecy Publishing Limited, 2015

London Docklands – A Strategic Plan, Docklands Joint Committee, 1976

London's Disused Underground Stations, J.E.Connor, Capital Transport, 2021

London's Lost Railways, Charles Klapper, Routledge & Kegan Paul, 1976

London Underground Rolling Stock, Brian Hardy, Capital Transport (various editions)

London Underground Rolling Stock Guide (ABC), Ben Muldoon, Ian Allan, 2014

London Underground Stations, David Leboff, Ian Allan, 1994

London Transport Railways Handbook, Gregory D. Beecroft, Iain D.O. Frew, Alan Holmewood, Barry Rayner and Barry Stevenson, The Foxley Press, 1983

London Transport Scrapbook for 1979, James Whiting, Capital Transport, 1980

London's Transport, Donal Murray, 2018

London Transport and the Politicians, Paul E. Garbutt, Ian Allan, 1985

London's Transport and the Olympics: Preparation, delivery and legacy, Malcolm Batten, Amberley Publishing, 2022

London's Underground, John Glover, Ian Allan (various editions)

Lost Underground Stations, John Glover, Crecy Publishing Limited, 2014

New Connections, David Mackay, Royal Academy of Arts

Public Transport in London – a regional approach, Greater London Council, 1972

Rails Through the Clay, D.F. Croome & Alan A. Jackson, Capital Transport, 1993

Railway Track Diagrams – Southern and TfL, Myles Munsey, TRACKmaps, 2019

The Architecture of the Jubilee Line Extension, David Bennett, Thomas Telford Books, 2004

The Jubilee Line, London Transport, 1979

The Jubilee Line, Mike Horne, Capital Transport, 2000

The London Underground, Andrew Emmerson, Shire Publications, 2010

The London Underground Tube Stock, J. Graeme Bruce, Ian Allan, 1988

The London Underground – An Illustrated History, Oliver Green, Ian Allan, 1987

The Railways of London's Docklands, Jonathan Willis, Pen and Sword, 2022

Underground Official Handbook, Piers Connor, Capital Transport, 1990

Underground Official Handbook, Bob Bayman, Capital Transport, 2008

Why do Shepherds need a Bush?, David Hilliam, The History Press, 2015

Reports

A railway plan for London, British Railways Board and London Transport Board, 1965
County of London Plan, J.H. Forshaw and P. Abercrombie, London County Council, 1943
Railway (London Plan) Committee 1944 – Report to the Minister of War Transport, Ministry of Transport, 1946
Railway (London Plan) Committee 1944 – Final Report to the Minister of Transport, Ministry of Transport, 1948
London Plan Working Party – Report to the Minister of Transport, British Transport Commission, 1949
Railways for London, Peter Kay, Campaign to Improve London's Transport
The London Rail Study – Part 1 and Part 2 (The Barran Report), Greater London Council / Department of the Environment, 1974
The Central London Rail Study, Department of Transport, 1989
Transport 2025, Transport for London, 2006
London Transport Annual Report, London Transport (various)
Jubilee Line Extension Information Pack, London Underground
The Jubilee Line, E.W. Cuthbert, Institute of Civil Engineers, 1979

The London Railway Record Magazine

'Early Jubilee Line Extension Plans', Jonathan James, Connor & Butler, No 20, July 1999
'Accommodating the Jubilee Line Extension', Les Collings, Connor & Butler, No 38, January 2004
'The London Plan', Jonathan James, Connor & Butler, No 65, October 2010
'The 1974 London Rail Study', Jonathan James, Peter Butler, No 71, April 2012
'The Central London Rail Study 1988/89', Jonathan James, Stepjump Design Limited, No 80, July 2014

Magazines and Newspapers

'London's Railway Plan', London Transport Magazine, London Transport, Volume 3, No 5, August 1949
Underground News, London Underground Railway Society, various issues
'Jubilee Line Extension', *Modern Railways Supplement*, March 2000
London Daily News, 9 April 1987
Modern Railways, Ian Allan, September 1970
Railways South East, Volume 1, No 3, Capital Transport, Winter 1988/89
Railways South East, Volume 2, No 1, Capital Transport, Winter 1989/90

Maps

The London Underground – A Diagrammatic History, Douglas Rose, Capital Transport, various editions
London Transport Railway Track Map, John Yonge and Trevor Haynes, Quail Map Co, 1981

An original painting of the proposed station at Millwall. (Karen Brown)

Other books you might like:

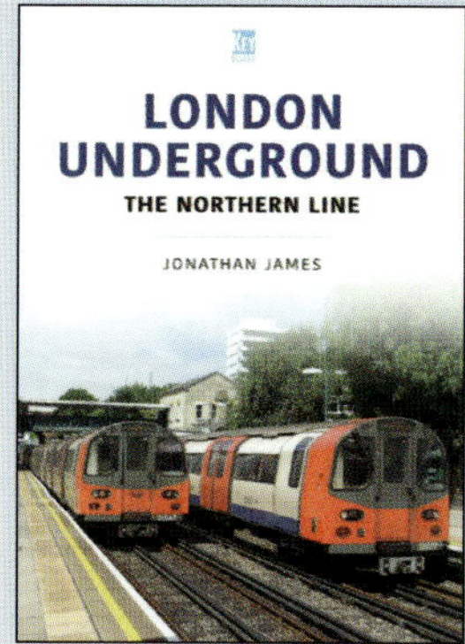

Transport Systems Series,
Vol. 9

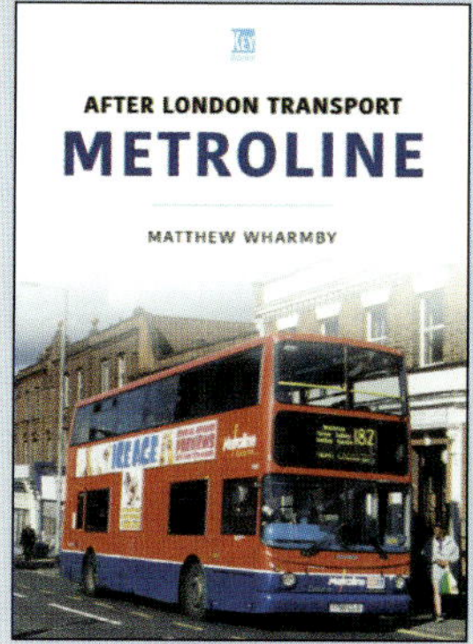

Transport Systems Series,
Vol. 11

Transport Systems Series,
Vol. 12

Transport Systems Series,
Vol. 13

Transport Systems Series,
Vol. 14

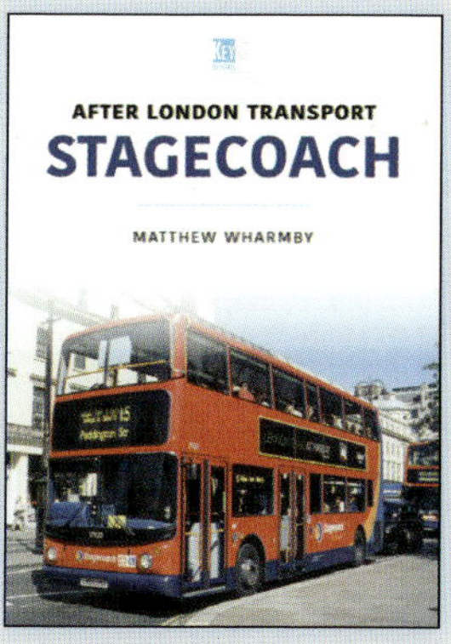

Transport Systems Series,
Vol. 15

For our full range of titles please visit:
shop.keypublishing.com/books

VIP Book Club

Sign up today and receive
TWO FREE E-BOOKS

Be the first to find out about our forthcoming
book releases and receive exclusive offers.

Register now at keypublishing.com/vip-book-club

*Our VIP Book Club is a 100% spam-free zone, and we will never share your email with anyone else.
You can read our full privacy policy at: privacy.keypublishing.com*